THE STORY OF A FLAG

Borgo Press Books by ADOLPHE D'ENNERY

The Children of Captain Grant (with Jules Verne)
Faust
The Story of a Flag
The Voyage Through the Impossible (with Jules Verne)

THE STORY OF A FLAG

AN EPIC DRAMA OF THE NAPOLEONIC WARS: A PLAY IN TWELVE SCENES

ADOLPHE D'ENNERY

Translated and Adapted by Frank J. Morlock

THE BORGO PRESS
MMXIII

THE STORY OF A FLAG

Copyright © 2009, 2013 by Frank J. Morlock

FIRST BORGO PRESS EDITION

Published by Wildside Press LLC

www.wildsidebooks.com

DEDICATION

For my dear friend, Victor Lantang—
for many years of friendship

CONTENTS

CAST OF CHARACTERS	9
SCENE I	13
SCENE II	46
SCENE III	70
SCENE IV	74
SCENE V	80
SCENE VI	90
SCENE VII	108
SCENE VIII	129
SCENE IX	156
SCENE X	174
SCENE XI	203
SCENE XII	213
ABOUT THE AUTHOR	214

CAST OF CHARACTERS

FRANÇOIS BEAUDOIN

FRÉDÉRIC WOLF

BONAPARTE

MOLINCHON

BOUDINIER

ANDRÉ

SATURNIN RENAUD

THE PREFECT

ANTOINE

THE SHEIK

MARSHALL NEY

GENERAL VAUBOIS

LANNES

AUSTRIAN COLONEL

A FIFER

A BOURGEOIS

FRENCH CAPTAIN

AUSTRIAN OFFICER

SECOND AUSTRIAN OFFICER

A COSSACK COMMANDER

A FRENCH SOLDIER

A MAN OF THE PEOPLE

A FRENCH COMMANDER

MADAME WOLF

ANTOINETTE

MARIE

LOUISE

JEANNE

GERTRUDE

NINA

A YOUNG SOLDIER

FRENCH SERGEANTS-MAJOR, FRENCH SOLDIERS, ZOUAVES, IMPERIAL GUARDS, EGYPTIANS, MAMELUKES, COSSACKS, CITIZENS OF VIENNA, GRENOBLE, AUSTRIANS

SCENE I

A workshop for embroidery.

MADAME WOLF

Come on, come on! Let's not waste time. Think that the work is urgent and we are behindhand.

MARIE

It's true, citizeness, but we are doing our best.

MADAME WOLF

It's not you I'm speaking to, child. I'm scolding you rather for being too worn out.

GERTRUDE (with irony)

Citizeness Wolf never has reproaches for Marie, she keeps them all for us. Marie is her favorite.

ALL

Oh, it's true, it's really true.

MADAME WOLF

You are unfair, Genevieve. If I have praise for her and remonstrances for you, the reason is quite simple. Look in the mirror and it will reply to you. Here's what it will say to you. Your eyes are shining and lively, your cheeks are white and rosy, because you slept well all night, and the whole evening before—while her features are tired from staying up.

LOUISE

Oh, it's not work alone which reddens her eyes and makes her pale.

MARIE

Louise!

MADAME WOLF

What do you mean? Speak, will you, I insist on it!

LOUISE

Well

JEANNE (low)

Shut up!

LOUISE (low)

We'll avenge ourselves later on the pretty favorite.

ANTOINETTE (outside)

No, no, no. I don't want any more—I've had enough of it.

(she enters)

MADAME WOLF

What's the matter with you, Antoinette?

ANTOINETTE

What's the matter with me? Madame asks what's the matter with me?

MADAME WOLF

First of all you know not to say "Madame."

ANTOINETTE

Yes, I know it's not said anymore, but I use it. As for me, I do not adhere to the current regime. I'm an aristocrat. Let them take my head, but they won't force me to speak.

JEANNE

But Antoinette, you'll end by compromising us all.

ANTOINETTE

That doesn't matter to me, I sacrificed your lives.

LOUISE

Thanks a lot!

ANTOINETTE

My principles above all! I won't tolerate a state of things like this any longer.

They even want to take my name from me, Antoinette and substitute that of Échalotte! (to Louise)

Citiziness Échalotte! Me, never—rather take my head.

LOUISE

But what do you want them to do with your head?

ANTOINETTE

What! What do I want them to do with it? I say they can take it. But watch out the first one to touch it.

MARIE

Look, what happened to you?

LOUISE

Where's your anger coming from this morning?

ANTOINETTE

Where's it coming from? It's coming from La Halle!

ALL

From La Halle!

MADAME WOLF

Come on, explain yourself.

ANTOINETTE

So be it. Madame had—

MADAME WOLF

Citizeness!

ANTOINETTE

Never in life. Madame had confided in me—

ALL

Ah!

ANTOINETTE

Madame had confided in me eight hundred thousand pounds. I was proud of this trust.

LOUISE

Well?

ANTOINETTE

I wanted to purchase a chicken, cutlets, and a liter of small peas.

LOUISE

Well?

ANTOINETTE

Well, they wanted three hundred for the chicken and six hundred for six veal cutlets.

MADAME WOLF

Why, that's the price.

ANTOINETTE

The price! Come on, will you, I know the price. My mother was a merchant in La Halle, and in those days for three hundred pounds I would have had three hundred chickens, and for six hundred pounds I could have purchased six calves.

MADAME WOLF (laughing)

Calm down.

ANTOINETTE

And these little peas at four hundred pounds a liter! That makes peas twenty sous apiece.

MADAME WOLF

But my poor Antoinette, it's not the price of goods that's increased, it's the value of assignats that's diminished.

ANTOINETTE

Isn't 500 written here?

(showing an assignat)

ALL

Yes.

ANTOINETTE

Then it's worth 500 since it's imprinted.

MADAME WOLF

Go to the kitchen for God's sake and try to make some lunch for us.

ANTOINETTE

I'm going there, Madame. But when I think that I'm going to fry twenty-five or thirty thousand pounds in my casseroles it breaks my heart, Madame—

MADAME WOLF

Citiziness, will you, wretch!

ANTOINETTE

Yes, Madame.

(Wolf comes in)

WOLF

If you don't give up your mania for calling us "sir" and "madame, I'm going to kick you out.

ANTOINETTE

Suffice, sir

(she goes out)

WOLF

Decidedly, mother, that girl is impossible. She'll wind up compromising us.

MADAME WOLF

Bah, it's no longer '93, and the Directory is less terrible than the Committee on Public Safety.

WOLF

All the same, I'd prefer to live far from here.

MADAME WOLF

Would you abandon your country?

WOLF

Do you condemn those who have left it, Citiziness? The nobles fled it leaving behind them children without protection. Weren't they more guilty? At least, I would take my mother with me.

MARIE

To properly judge those of whom you speak, you'd need to know the reasons for their actions.

MADAME WOLF

Yes, yes, quite imperious. Some separations caused bitter tears to be shed.

(Marie lowers her head and weeps)

WOLF

That's possible, but after all, is it really my country that I'd be leaving? I was born on the frontier. Sometimes our village belongs to France, sometimes to Germany. So that in truth, I don't know if, French today, I won't be German tomorrow.

MARIE

And doesn't your heart tell you which is your true country?

MADAME WOLF

Is the memory of your father erased from your memory?

WOLF

My father?

MADAME WOLF

He was a brave officer in the service of France.

WOLF

What has France done for us since we lost him? Nothing, therefore, I owe it nothing. My country will be the one where I shall live calm and happy. You ask me what my heart thinks? Well, the country it will adopt will be that of my wife and my children. and to speak frankly again, Citiziness, I will tell you, that for the last three years my mother has made of you almost my sister, that she has succeeded so well in causing me to share her tenderness, if you wish, we shall always live with her, and it's you that I will allow, mistress of me to say one day, "Frédéric, here's where our children will grow up, here's where our country will be."

MARIE (trembling)

Frédéric!

MADAME WOLF

Speak, my child.

MARIE

Frédéric, your mother has taken me in. You've become my brother, she's covered me with kindness, my heart is full of the most lively gratitude. In me you'll find, she, a devoted daughter, you, a sister. But only a sister.

WOLF (with spite)

You hear her, mother. (Angrily) Oh, I read her heart correctly, it's not me she loves.

MADAME WOLF

My son—

WOLF (aside)

Bad luck to the one she prefers to me.

JÉRÔME (entering)

Hello, everybody. (noticing Madame Wolf) Oh, Citizeness.

MADAME WOLF

Hello, my lad.

JÉRÔME (embarrassed)

Citizeness, I came to find out if the embroidery is progressing.

(looking at Marie)

MADAME WOLF

Yes, yes, it will soon be ready.

SATURNIN (entering)

Servant, little citizenesses.

(seeing Madame Wolf)

Citizeness.

WOLF (to his mother)

Yet another one who didn't expect to find you here.

MADAME WOLF (laughing)

It's true. (aloud) What brings you here, my lad?

SATURNIN (looking at Louise)

Citizeness—I—I—came to learn if—if the embroidery is coming along.

WOLF

Him, too.

FRANÇOIS

Greetings to all. (noticing Madame Wolf) Oh, Citizeness Wolf. Hello, Citizen Wolf. I came—I came—

WOLF

You want to know if the embroidery is coming, right?

FRANÇOIS

If the embroidery is coming. Yes, exactly.

(looks at Jeanne)

WOLF

It's singular. All three for the same reason.

FRANÇOIS (low to Marie)

Citizeness, I need to speak to you, here, right away.

MARIE (low)

That's impossible.

FRANÇOIS

It concerns my happiness, my life. You will come, won't you?

WOLF

He's whispering to her.

JEANNE (who listened)

A rendezvous. Here. Soon.

WOLF

Ah, indeed. What the devil are you knitting, really, that interests these three citizens so much?

FRANÇOIS

What are they embroidering? It's a flag.

WOLF

A flag?

FRANÇOIS

Yes, the rumor has spread the last few days that the brave army of Italy has fought an enemy whose forces increase from day to day, and that the hero of Montenotte, Lodi, and Mantua was placed in a dangerous situation by the approach of a new army under the command of General Aloizi. Soon our hearts were moved, three thousand braves, three thousand volunteers presented themselves ready to leave, and it's this flag they are going to fight under, that the citizenesses are knitting at the moment.

WOLF

Well! And you?

FRANÇOIS

We are working on it also.

WOLF

What, all three?

JÉRÔME

Yes, surely.

SATURNIN

Me, I'm a silk-weaver. I've weaved the material of three colors.

JÉRÔME

As for me, I'm a carver, and I've carved the pole of the most solid wood.

FRANÇOIS

And, I chiseled the lance which surmounts it, and which will wait for the enemy, facing him.

JÉRÔME

You see, citizenesses, this flag is our child, and today is the day of its birth.

FRANÇOIS

This bit of material you are embroidering, young girls,—thousands of men will die fighting for the glory of planting it on a fortification, to unfurl it, triumphant, in the midst of an enemy capitol.

WOLF

And yet it will still be only a bit of silk, a bit of wood, and copper.

FRANÇOIS

Yes, when it leaves our hands—but once it passes into the hands of our braves, once it floats over a battlefield, it will soon transform itself, it will seem as if it's alive, as if it breathes, as if it dreams—

(gentle music)

ALL

It's true! It's true!

FRANÇOIS

Later, when the war's over, it will return, shredded by gun fire, and on its passage all heads will bow, all hearts will be moved, all eyes filled with tears—for its thousand wounds will tell of the thousand soldiers fallen in its defense, it will bear in its folds the honors and glory of the nation. The flag is the soul of the army, it's the paternal hearth which follows the distant soldier, it's the village clock which marches in the midst of a regiment, it's the absent fatherland, whether it be in the heart of the desert, in the ocean, or even at the end of the world, the flag is always

France.

WOLF (with irony)

I admire your enthusiasm, citizen.

FRANÇOIS

But you don't share it.

ANDRÉ (forcefully)

Lunch is ready.

MADAME WOLF

Come children.

ANDRÉ

Old man André who lives upstairs is asking to speak to Madame.

SATURNIN and JÉRÔME

André!

MADAME WOLF

Show him in, He's a poor man who likes my company.

MARIE

If you wish, citizeness, I'm going to receive him. I will come back right away.

FRANÇOIS (aside)

She will stay.

MADAME WOLF (low)

Yes, speak to him.. Besides, he's come for you, no question.

(to workers)

Goodbye, citizens.

FRANÇOIS

And the flag, citizeness?

MADAME WOLF

Our embroidery is completed. You can have it soon.

JÉRÔME

In that case, if you permit it, we will bring the tip, the shaft.

SATURNIN

I'll bring the tie.

MADAME WOLF

It's agreed. Au revoir.

(She goes, Wolf leaves followed by Antoinette)

ANTOINETTE (counting)

I added it up. They are going to devour 17,000 pounds for lunch.

(The seamstresses follow her)

LOUISE (low)

She asked to remain so as to be with him.

JEANNE (low)

We have to listen to them so as to confound them.

LOUISE (low)

And to avenge ourselves on her.

(they leave)

MARIE

You've got news, my friend. Is there some hope?

ANDRÉ

Alas, my child, what I conceive for you is still very flimsy.

MARIE

Speak! Speak!

ANDRÉ

Poor proscribed priest, forced to hide myself from all eyes, to conceal all pursuits, it's only with great difficulty I've been able to obtain information about your family.

MARIE

But you actually have some?

ANDRÉ

I've been assured that persons with your name crossed through Italy a few months ago. They must have settled themselves in Florence or Naples. Later, perhaps, we can get more certain information.

MARIE

I know what's become of my mother and my father. And it's to you that I owe this joy. Oh, how can I thank you.

FRANÇOIS

Marie.

ANDRÉ

Someone.

MARIE

Don't be afraid; he's a friend.

FRANÇOIS

Yes, a friend who would give his life for you, citizeness; a man of honor who'd sooner die than denounce this unfortunate.

ANDRÉ

Denounce me! What have I done?

FRANÇOIS

I know you, Father André. I know that you are an old priest who didn't want to leave France. Take my hand and look me in the face; you will understand that you have nothing to fear from me. I respect your holy ministry, as I must also respect in you your age. So fear nothing, be twice reassured Father. I bow before your grey hair, and I believe in God.

ANDRÉ

Be blessed, my son. Till soon, Marie.

(he leaves)

FRANÇOIS

Marie, it's for me that you remained. I thank you for it, from the bottom of my heart.

MARIE

Yes, it's for you, François

FRANÇOIS

You! What's it mean?

MARIE

They're waiting for me, you know. What have you to tell me?

FRANÇOIS

Marie, the work done almost in common, which allows me to speak to you sometimes. Now it's all over. What's going to become of me, now? Because you know perfectly well that I love you.

MARIE

Yes, I know, François. And yet you are speaking to me of this love for the first time. And it will also be the last.

FRANÇOIS

Why then I deceived myself when I dared to hope you would not refuse to join your fate to mine.

MARIE

This marriage is impossible.

FRANÇOIS

Impossible! Oh, Marie, Marie!

MARIE

Listen to me, my friend. You will judge later. My name is Marie de Marsilly.

FRANÇOIS

You are noble!

MARIE

My father is the Duke de Marsilly. Condemned to death three years ago by the Revolutionary Tribunal. My mother succeeded in eluding the investigations of our persecutors. We took refuge in Nantes; the excellent Madame Wolf consented to give us asylum. A prolonged stay might have compromised her, ruined her; we decided to expatriate ourselves, but on the day fixed for our departure, broken by sorrows, overwhelmed by so much emotion, I fell lifeless, dying in the doorway of the house, and for a week I placed those who were dear to me in peril.

FRANÇOIS

But they left, they were capable of abandoning you?

MARIE

Yes, they left. I was the one who forced them to flee.

FRANÇOIS

You?

MARIE

All efforts to tear them away from my bedside had been useless, and I, in my delirium, I always saw death threatening them. Fever gave me strength. I rushed out of my bed, weeping, begging, "If you stay, I'm leaving," I screamed. "I'm leaving this very moment. And, dressing hurriedly, I rushed toward the door. "You will kill her, "said the Doctor, "You are killing her." My father stretched suppliant hands towards me, my mother was on her knees; I think she was weeping. "Leave," I said to them, "or rather stay and see me die." Only my mother replied. "Marie, we will go." She got up calm and strong because I was wrong, she wasn't crying, she was praying.

FRANÇOIS

Finish, finish, Marie.

MARIE

The next day was a very sad day. It wasn't a separation well submitted to, they returned; they kept returning; we separated twenty times that day.

FRANÇOIS

And since then, they wrote to you? You know where they are?

MARIE

Alas, Carrier, from the Committee on Public Safety, came to Nantes; his suspicions already threatened my benefactress; she changed her name and we came to Paris, where we've been for the last three years. No doubt my family has tried to find me, but this name change, and this place change have rendered their efforts useless. Now, François, you know my secret. You know I have the right to dispose of myself without the consent of my father.

FRANÇOIS

I understand you, Marie. Goodbye, all my beautiful hopes, all my fine dreams! Alas, my sweet illusions are vanishing.

MARIE

François.

FRANÇOIS

I am quite unlucky and I always will be.

MARIE

No. Someone else will console you.

FRANÇOIS

Someone else? Ah, you don't even suspect with what love I love you. No, you don't understand this tenderness without limits which make you the only dream of my life. Another, you said? From those that surround you? Ah, hold on. That thought makes them odious to me! I cannot aspire to your heart; I understand it, I feel it, but I would die a thousand times before my mouth would be able to say to Another, that oath that I took at your feet, Marie,—until my last day, you will be my only love, my unique hope! Oh, Marie, I love you—I love you.

MARIE

You're wrong, François, there are nice and beautiful young girls here; they accuse me of pride because sad memories often make me silent. They envy the affection Madame Wolf has for me, not knowing the price I've paid for it with misfortunes. In the end, they don't love me, but I love them; I know their souls well, and know they would say to me "Let's be friends," that they'd stretch out their hands to me if I could open my heart to them.

LOUISE (sadly)

Miss de Marsilly.

MARIE

You?

LOUISE

Would you allow us to be your friends?

MARIE

What? You were there?

LOUISE

We were very guilty because we were listening.

JEANNE

Do you refuse to forgive us? Do you refuse? (she offers her hand)

MARIE (talking her hand and pulling her to her heart)

Ah, I knew perfectly well it would suffice to know me to give me a place there.

(embracing the others)

And that you would become my friends, my sisters.

LOUISE

Yes, your sisters. Faithful and devoted, and you, François, keep your love, she alone is worthy of it. She is noble by her birth, be more so by your actions and your names may be joined as your hearts already are.

FRANÇOIS (to Louise)

I will take your advice. Yes, I will raise myself up, Marie. How? I don't know yet, but I intend to do it and it will happen.

(noise of drums outside.)

WOLF

What's going on?

MADAME WOLF

What's this uproar?

JÉRÔME (entering with Saturnin)

Citizeness—the flag?

MADAME WOLF

What's this mean?

SATURNIN

It means that the volunteers are impatient to leave, and they've sent a detachment to come get the flag!

MADAME WOLF

Quick then, my children!

FRANÇOIS

It lacks the cock.

JÉRÔME

I brought my pole.

SATURNIN

And my tie-cord.

FRANÇOIS

But it still lacks the fer-de-lance.

JÉRÔME

I brought the lamé from your workshop as I passed.

FRANÇOIS

In that case all that remains is for me to attach the material.

MARIE

François—it still lacks something.

FRANÇOIS

What do you mean?

MARIE

To tell you of all those who will expose their lives to defend it. It seems to me that if it were blessed, the blessing of the flag would extend to all its defenders.

FRANÇOIS

I understand you, Marie. Hold on, hold on.

(François leaves. Clamor under the window)

WOLF

What impatience! They are very turbulent, your friends.

JÉRÔME

I'm going to speak to them.

(at window)

In a moment, comrades, it will be finished.

VOICES (outside)

Bravo! Hurry it up!

WOLF (low)

François was here, near her. I wasn't mistaken. He's the one she loves.

ANDRÉ

What do you want with me, citizen? Why'd you bring me here?

FRANÇOIS

I am going to tell you. This flag that they just finished is all our work, it's almost our child. Those that you see here are brave workers who have not driven all religious feeling from their souls! I ask you to call on our child the blessing of heaven.

ANDRÉ

I am ready. And I read in your hearts that you knew my secret though I thought you were unaware of it.

ALL

Ah!

ANDRÉ

Yes, you know who I am, and here I am prepared to respond to your desire; I wish it, I owe it, because I was without asylum, you opened your arms to me, I was without bread, you shared yours with me; I am proscribed, and you've respected my secret; I am your brother, and the flag of the nation will always be mine.

(turning towards the flag)

I bless you in the name of the Lord, Flag of France, noble symbol. Almighty God, you who are also the God of Armies, extend your protective hand over all those who follow this standard. Lead them from victory to victory, let them soon give to our unfortunate country a glorious leader who will return to France its splendor, religion to its altars, and exiles to their hearths. Yet once more, flag of France, I bless you in the name of the Lord.

FRANÇOIS

And now it lacks nothing.

(uproar outside)

SATURNIN (at the window)

Calm down, comrades, it's ready— Behold!

ALL

Ah!

FRANÇOIS (going to Marie)

Marie, if I succeed in making the humble name that I bear illustrious—won't you allow me to hope?

MARIE (low)

I cannot promise to be yours.

(reaction by François)

But I swear to you I won't belong to any others.

FRANÇOIS

Thanks. I will succeed.

WOLF (to François)

Perhaps, Citizen, perhaps.

FRANÇOIS

What are you saying?

WOLF

That I hate you because you love Marie.

FRANÇOIS

You! You!

WOLF

And between us, it's war to the death.

FRANÇOIS

Well, so be it! War!

(Volunteers enter)

FIRST VOLUNTEER

Well, Citizeness, our flag?

SECOND VOLUNTEER

We are impatient to leave.

ALL

Yes! Yes!

(with admiration)

Ah!

FRANÇOIS

Our flag, our child! It's strange how, looking at it now, I feel my heart beat violently. Well, Citizen Wolf—is it still only a little stick of wood, a bit of leather and silk? Look, barely adjusted, it stands up proudly, it's the lifeless body which a soul just entered!

(seizing the flag)

Yes, it lives, I feel it palpitate under my hand! It speaks, I hear what it says to me. Glory, Country, Liberty! It marches, I feel it pull me! Well, I will follow you, noble standard; my career is chosen, my future laid out, and I will not leave you. I'm a soldier.

ALL

Bravo!

JÉRÔME

Me neither, I don't want to leave it. François, I'm leaving with you.

SATURNIN (weeping)

Say, the rest of you, am I not its father, too? Well! I'm making myself a soldier like you.

ANTOINETTE

Damn it all! I'm electrified! I really want to be a soldier, too.

FRANÇOIS

We'll tour the world with it.

(pointing to the flag)

Friends! Behold the one who will lead us to victory! We are going to tour the world with it!

ALL

Viva! Viva!

CURTAIN

SCENE II

A military camp on the plateau of Rivoli.

AT RISE, soldiers of the Vaubois Division are on stage.

JÉRÔME

Well, comrades! Our small reinforcements arrived just in time.

SATURNIN

It seems the army is not content, and it is indeed right to complain, abandoned as it is by the Directory.

JÉRÔME

It's true. Bonaparte has no more than 36,000 men to fight 90,000 Austrians.

SATURNIN

Do you know what the soldiers are saying? After having destroyed two armies sent against us, we still failed to destroy those who were opposed to our troops on the Rhine. Beaulieu succeeded Wurmser, Alvinczi, Wurmser, and they abandon us to be taken by two numberless armies; they want that, beaten at last, crushed by numbers, we return without honor and without glory, as if we had not done our duty.

JÉRÔME

All those surrounding us are part of the division of Vaubois. They were forced to withdraw from the city of Trent, to pass through Adige, and here we are occupying the plateau of Rivoli.

SATURNIN

Look how downtrodden, discouraged, they are. There's only one man who can raise their energy!

JÉRÔME

Bonaparte!

SATURNIN

Yes, but he's at Vicenza holding the head of General Alvinczi, who commands an army three times more considerable than his.

(Roll of drums. All stand.)

JÉRÔME

Inspection.

(Boudinier and Molinchon enter from different directions.)

BOUDINIER

We have kitchen duty. That humiliates me, Mr. Molinchon.

MOLINCHON

And that's the cause that humiliates you, Mr. Boudinier.

BOUDINIER

Because you are only a coward.

MOLINCHON

Ah!

BOUDINIER

And I have the blood of heroes in my veins.

MOLINCHON

That's not my fault, Mr. Boudinier. Courage—it is not at command.

BOUDINIER

And why are you afraid? You haven't yet seen fire.

MOLINCHON

Nor have you, Mr. Boudinier.

BOUDINIER

No, but I am burning to see it. I know what it will do to me because when I think of it, my hands shiver, prickles in my arms, pins and needles in my legs! I have the desire to kill, what! Oh, I will eat ten enemies by myself, alone—with weapons and equipment.

MOLINCHON

Not me. I don't have as much appetite as that.

BOUDINIER

By Jove!

MOLINCHON

The idea of battle arouses in me something I cannot tell you.

BOUDINIER

I know what it is.

MOLINCHON

And then I experience a strong desire to run; I don't know if it is to the rear, but I think it is not forward.

BOUDINIER

Come on, you are no more courageous than a rabbit. And as for me, I am a tiger.

MOLINCHON

That's possible, Mr. Boudinier, but it's independent of my wishes. When I think of myself facing a cannon ball, I immediately seek some place it could do me less harm.

BOUDINIER

And what place have you chosen?

MOLINCHON

It's still in your stomach that it would be less agreeable to me.

BOUDINIER

Come on, you are nothing at all.

MOLINCHON

But it's not my fault if I don't have the heart of a hero like you.

ANTOINETTE (as a vivandière)

And as for me, I don't love heroes!

BOUDINIER

Antoinette!

MOLINCHON

Citizeness Éscalotte.

ANTOINETTE

I no longer call myself Éscalotte.

BOUDINIER

Will it be soon, Citizeness Antoinette, that you will choose a husband from among the two of us?

MOLINCHON

You know how I idolize you, Éscalotte!

ANTOINETTE

I just told you that I no longer call myself Éscalotte, I peeled this name off under the flags.

BOUDINIER

Be it under one name or another, you are no less agreeable, Antoinette.

ANTOINETTE

Right. That's sweet, that is. And it's said by a brave, and I won't bestow my heart except in favor of a brave.

BOUDINIER (fatuously)

I will be her lucky conqueror.

ANTOINETTE

Ah, it's not you, conscript Molinchon, who will find these things.

MOLINCHON

I find many pretty things, Éscalotte.

ANTOINETTE

And why don't you say them?

MOLINCHON

I don't dare.

ANTOINETTE

Hum! Said by a Frenchman, and doesn't dare anything!— It's a waste of time to inspect from hour to hour, they won't find us more numerous.

SECOND SOLDIER

Nor less discouraged.

JÉRÔME

Come on, come on, comrades. We won't let ourselves be beaten down, what the devil!

ANTOINETTE

You are newcomers, the rest of you, you haven't been present at our battles, you don't know the sorrow, the humiliation, of beating a retreat after so many victories.

SOLDIERS

It's true! It's true!

(noises off)

CAPTAIN

What's that?

MOLINCHON

Captain, one would say two women have just arrived in the camp.

ANTOINETTE

What? What would one say?

CAPTAIN

Two women— Have them brought here.

(Molinchon leaves and returns with Marie and Madame Wolf)

CAPTAIN

Who are you?

MADAME WOLF

Two women traveling under the protection of God.

CAPTAIN

Where are you coming from? What are your names?

MARIE

We're coming from Paris.

JÉRÔME

That voice.

MARIE

My name is—

JÉRÔME

Citizeness Marie! It's she! Marie!

MARIE

Citizen Jérôme.

MADAME WOLF

Him!

CAPTAIN

You know these two women?

JÉRÔME

Yes, I know them!

ANTOINETTE

Me, too! I fed her enough.

SATURNIN

Yes, my Captain, yes, we all know them; Jérôme and I, and François.

François's going to be very happy.

MARIE

François is here isn't he?

JÉRÔME

Yes, citizeness.

CAPTAIN

In that case, you can vouch for these two citizenesses?

JÉRÔME

Heart for heart, my Captain. Eh, hold on, you want to know who they are. Their hands embroidered our flag.

CAPTAIN

That's good enough. I am leaving you, citizenesses. When you want to continue your journey, the Lieutenant will escort you out of the camp.

(the Captain leaves)

MARIE

But him! Him?

JÉRÔME

François? Hey, hold on. There he is.

(calling)

François! François!

FRANÇOIS

What's wrong?

JÉRÔME

Luck, comrade.

FRANÇOIS

What are you saying? What do I see, Marie?

Darling Marie!

MARIE

My friend!

FRANÇOIS

Ah, you were right, Jérôme, a great piece of luck! Marie, darling Marie, is it heaven that sent you? Yes, yes, that's what guided you. It's heaven that permits, on the eve of battle, that I see you one more time.

MARIE (with fright)

A battle!

FRANÇOIS

Oh, don't tremble, don't worry for us, Marie; we've all three sworn to distinguish ourselves in the shadow of our flag, and we await battle like a day of joy and festivity.

SATURNIN

It's true! But tell us, what's become of Citizeness Louise?

JÉRÔME

And Citizeness Jeanne?

MARIE

They are still in Paris.

MADAME WOLF

They are thinking of you. They are praying for you.

MARIE

And they are waiting for you.

JÉRÔME

The brave girls.

SATRUNIN

We will see them again, my friends, we will see them again.

JÉRÔME

François is luckier than we are.

FRANÇOIS

Who knows? Perhaps this voyage whose cause I am ignorant of may be a source of chagrin for me. Marie, how does it happen that you left Paris?

MARIE

My duty was to brave all dangers to find my family.

FRANÇOIS

Do you have some clues?

MARIE

Yes, we learned that my mother and my father are locked up in Genoa during the war.

MADAME WOLF

And since that day, Marie had only one desire; to leave for Genoa—but to go alone was impossible.

MARIE

She left everything to accompany me.

MADAME WOLF

I didn't leave anything, I didn't abandon anyone to follow you.

FRANÇOIS

What do you mean?

MADAME WOLF

Am I not alone in the world?

FRANÇOIS

Alone?

JÉRÔME

What are you saying?

MARIE

Poor woman.

SATURNIN

And Wolf?

FRANÇOIS

Your son?

MADAME WOLF

Oh, don't mention him to me. Don't even pronounce his name.

ALL

Why?

MADAME WOLF

I say that his birth was a misfortune, as his life is a shame. I say it: it would be better I were dead than to have given him life.

FRANÇOIS

What fault has he committed?

MADAME WOLF

A fault? Say a crime!

JÉRÔME

A crime!

MADAME WOLF

Yes, the most horrible, the most infamous, the most cowardly of crimes, do you understand at last? He not only abandoned his mother, he has—

FRANÇOIS (forcefully)

He has betrayed his country?

MADAME WOLF

Indeed, he said he no longer had a country— And I—I no longer have a son!

FRANÇOIS (pointing to Marie)

You still have a daughter.

(taking hands with Jérôme and Saturnin)

And here are three soldiers who love you like a mother. You will become a mother!

MADAME WOLF

Thanks! Yes, all my family from now on.

JÉRÔME

But your son?

SATURNIN

What's become of him?

MARIE

He left France.

MADAME WOLF

He enlisted among our enemies. He's part of a foreign legion in the service of Austria.

ALL

Of Austria?

MADAME WOLF

Yes, a foreign legion. For even our enemies probably wouldn't have admitted him to their ranks.

FRANÇOIS

God prevent me from meeting him face to face.

MARIE (low)

That day you will remember his mother and you will have pity on her.

(aloud, seeing the Lieutenant return)

François, my friends, we are going to continue our voyage. You must say goodbye to us.

MADAME WOLF

No. Au revoir, my friends!

FRANÇOIS

Au revoir, au revoir, Marie!

MARIE

Others have flourished treading the road you are following; good courage, my friend, good courage.

(she offers her hand)

FRANÇOIS (pressing it in his)

But, if no one tells you soon, François Beaudoin has distinguished himself and got himself a rank— Say François is dead!

MADAME WOLF (to Lieutenant)

Citizen Lieutenant, we are at your disposal.

FRANÇOIS (to Madame Wolf)

Watch carefully over her.

MADAME WOLF

For who else would I live now?

FRANÇOIS

Au revoir, my dear Madame Wolf. Au revoir, Marie, au revoir.

MARIE (shaking his hand)

Au revoir—

ANTOINETTE

Damn, but this upsets me.

(Drum roll. Everyone grabs his weapon and all fall in)

VAUBOIS (arriving)

What's wrong?

CAPTAIN (arriving)

The General! The General-in-Chief just arrived in the camp.

VAUBOIS

Bonaparte, my friends. We are no longer abandoned. Bonaparte is among us.

ALL

Long live General Bonaparte!

BONAPARTE (arriving on horseback with his Sergeant-Major)

General Vaubois, you bravely attacked the position of Davidovich. You were going to be victorious when a panic terror spread through a part of your troops; your soldiers fled in disorder, they, whose bravery was formerly cited in the army.

VAUBOIS

General, I thought my duty was to fall back to this plateau, so as not to be cut off by the enemy.

BONAPARTE

You did well. But, you, soldiers, I am not satisfied with you. You displayed neither fortitude not discipline. You allowed yourself to be driven from your positions when a handful of brave men ought to have stopped an army. Soldiers of the 39th and 85th, you are not French Soldiers. Sergeant- Major, you will write on their flag, "They are no longer part of the Army of Italy."

ALL (in despair, groaning)

Ah!

ANTOINE (weeping with rage)

No, no. That cannot be! That won't be! A thousand times, no.

BONAPARTE

What are you saying?

FRANÇOIS

He says, General, that it would be better to kill them, make them die by their own arms, than to dishonor brave soldiers for their first fault.

SATURNIN and JÉRÔME

François!

BONAPARTE

Come forward and continue.

FRANÇOIS

General, they were outnumbered three to one and they had the weakness to retreat! Well, in the next battle, put all of us in your advance guard, let us be outnumbered ten to one, and you will see if we are worthy of being part of the Army of Italy.

ALL

Yes, yes, yes!

BONAPARTE

Wait. I will decide later.

FRANÇOIS

So be it, General, you will decide.

(He takes the flag and moves toward the rear)

BONAPARTE

What are you doing?

FRANÇOIS

General, we are volunteers, arrived just a few days ago. Our flag did not retreat before the enemy. Your sentence must not reach it.

BONAPARTE

That's fair!

(to François)

What's your name?

FRANÇOIS

François Beaudoin, Parisian volunteer.

BONAPARTE

I'll remember it.

FRANÇOIS

Long live the general!

SATURNIN and JÉRÔME

Long live Bonaparte!

BONAPARTE (getting off his horse)

Vaubois, send your men away.

(He goes into Vaubois's tent. The soldiers withdraw.)

BONAPARTE

I have no illusions. The army is discouraged. What a struggle!

If, at least, they gave us help proportionate to our risks! But, no—each day the number of our braves diminishes: Joubert, Lannes, Lamard, Murat, Chabrand are out of combat; their soldiers have been decimated by grapeshot.

VAUBOIS

And the Directory doesn't send reinforcements; it remains deaf to our complaints.

BONAPARTE

My letters have remained unanswered. Never mind. Tomorrow, we will act.

VAUBOIS (astonished)

Tomorrow!

BONAPARTE

Do you think I intend to give the army time to be further demoralized? No, no—if we can fight the enemy neither in the fortified positions he now occupies, nor in the plain where he has the advantage by deploying forces very superior to ours, we will astonish him by a bold plan. The skirmishers of Rome are caught in the midst of a swamp near Arcole. That's where I intend to attack the enemy, that's where we will attempt our last chance.

VAUBOIS

The skirmishers of Rome.

BONAPARTE

There are three dikes placed in the midst of the swamp. That terrain annuls the advantages of numbers. They cannot deploy on the dikes. The courage of the heads of our columns will decide the victory. Ah, if only I had a few thousand more men.

VOICES (outside)

General Bonaparte! General Bonaparte!

BONAPARTE

What do you want?

(Lannes enters with a large number of wounded and convalescent soldiers)

BONAPARTE

What do I see? Lannes?

LANNES

Yes, General Bonaparte, and all those able to leave hospital have come to form ranks around you.

BONAPARTE

What, my friends, my brave soldiers—

LANNES

News is spreading rapidly in the hospitals of Milan, of Cremona, of Lodi—the army is in peril. Yes, the army is in peril! So, you ought to have seen, general, those overcome by fever and serious wounds are rising from their beds of sorrow with looks of wrath, with threatening gestures, sick or wounded, all wanted to rejoin their flag, all have forgotten their suffering to think only of their country.!

BONAPARTE (shaking their hands)

Ah, brave hearts. Let the Directory abandon us. With such soldiers how to fear defeat!

(he gestures to Vaubois who moves away. A new Drum Roll. Bonaparte mounts his horse.)

BONAPARTE

Soldiers! I really want to forget your faults and only remember your exploits.

FRANÇOIS

Long live the General!

ALL (joyfully)

Long live the general!

BONAPARTE

I pardon you. You will march in the avante-garde. May victory come to absolve you further. I await you at Arcole!

ALL

To Arcole! To Arcole!

CURTAIN

SCENE III

A peasant hovel.

WOLF

Lieutenant, keep a strict watch over your men. Our foreign legion must not be accused of lack of discipline.

LIEUTENANT

Your orders will be strictly followed, Captain.

WOLF (sitting down)

And, I, too, François Beaudoin, I became a soldier to get closer to Marie, and we'll see which of the two of us reaches his goal first. Has he even won a sergeant's insignia? No. And here I am, a captain—in a foreign legion, it's true, but wasn't Marie's father noble? Hasn't he emigrated, meaning like me, he adopted another country? The cause I'm engaged to serve is his! The party of the old monarchy is powerful. I will succeed, and if Sergeant or Lieutenant Baudoin has going for him the heart or romantic mind of Marie, Colonel or General Wolf will place in the balance the will of the Count of Marsilly. Yes, yes, Marie will belong to me, and when peace is made, I will return to France, rich, envied. (sadly) Envied, but who will love me? And the day of my departure she extended her hand toward me, her mouth opened to curse me. Oh, well, she's my mother and she will forget.

COLONEL (entering)

Any news, Captain?

WOLF

None, Colonel.

COLONEL

Truly, the French have a strange way of making war. They tell us they're engaged in the middle of a swamp that surrounds us. Singular battlefield.

WOLF

Pardon, Colonel, I don't see any other which offers them chances of success.

COLONEL

What do you mean?

WOLF

We have forty thousand men, the French merely thirteen thousand; their general has chosen this swamp, because when fighting on dikes numbers are no longer an advantage.

COLONEL

Meaning we don't equal them in bravery!

WOLF

I am certain they will soon have proof to the contrary.

AIDE DE CAMP (presenting a dispatch)

A message for you, sir.

COLONEL

Let me see. (opening and reading)

An order for us to cross back into the village of Arcole, to fortify the bridge and to interdict the passage of the enemy army— That's fine. Tell the General that the French will attempt vainly to cross the bridge.

(The Aide de Camp salutes and leaves)

WOLF

Pardon, Colonel. Do you know what corps is advancing against us?

COLONEL

The division of Augereau.

WOLF

The division of Augereau. So much the better. It's well they are part of it.

COLONEL

What are you talking about?

WOLF

Men that I hate most in the world. There's one of them especially that I'm eager to meet.

AIDE DE CAMP (returning)

Colonel, the French are approaching. The General orders that the columns fall back on Arcole. He's confiding the defense of the bridge to your regiment. The artillery will support you.

COLONEL

Come, Captain, come.

(A distant roll of drums. They leave.)

CURTAIN

SCENE IV

The bridge at Arcole.

AT RISE, a detachment of French marksmen enters, among them Antoine, Molinchon, and Boudinier.

MOLINCHON (calmly)

Ah, now that it's starting I am sure that fear is going to run straight through me,

ANTOINE

Come on, come on, conscripts, to work

(firing a shot)

BOUDINIER (very pale and trembling)

Yes, yes, to—to—to work.

ANTOINE

Fire!

BOUDINIER

Yes, yes—gre—grenadier.

MOLINCHON

Is Mr. Boudinier lucky to be brave.

ANTOINE

(loading his weapon)

Fire, will you!

MOLINCHON

Ah, by Jove, fire. That's not very easy. (firing) Heavens, I got one. Your turn, Mr. Boudinier.

BOUDINIER

Yes, m-my turn.

(he fires and starts trembling, then looks around uneasily)

MOLINCHON

(loading his weapon)

What funny courage you have, Mr. Boudinier!

ANTOINE

It has a devilish resemblance to fear.

(Return fire from the Austrians)

MOLINCHON

Ah, why they are going to do us harm, those guys, Mr. Boudinier?

BOUDINIER

Eh! What is it you want to do about it?

MOLINCHON

I will never have the courage to allow myself to shoot like that. I'm not very brave. I prefer to go forward to exterminate them to make them shut up.

BOUDINIER

Is—is that dumb, really!

ANTOINE

Well! There's a coward who's not far from being a brave man.

MOLINCHON

Ah, what's that?

ANTOINE

The Austrians are occupying the bridge. I recognize them. It's the Metrouski Division. It's going to get warm, gang, it's going to get warm. Let's fall back on that column.

BOUDINIER

Yes, yes, let's fall back.

MOLINCHON

It's off-pissing to fall back.

(The Austrians spread out on the bridge. The noise of drums and ballet music. The battle begins with vigor. A lot of Austrians commanded by the Colonel and Wolf attack them In the middle of the battle the flag falls. Wolf and François notice it at the same time and both rush towards it. They see and recognize each other.)

FRANÇOIS

Fredric Wolf.

WOLF

François.

FRANÇOIS

Dare to touch it, will you! Dare, will you, to lay a sacrilegious hand on the flag of your country!

WOLF

It's the one Marie embroidered, it's the one you swore to defend. I intend that as you die, you'll see it in my hands.

(Wolf stands to strike at François with his sword. François snatches it from him and casts it at some distance, then seizes the flag and points the tip at Wolf.)

FRANÇOIS

Today's not the day it will endure the shame of being raised by you. Rally to me, Parisians!

(Jérôme, Saturnin and several soldiers surround him. The battle rages Anew. The Austrians are pushed back and cross the bridge. Augereau rushes up in pursuit of them, after having drowned a large number.)

AUGEREAU

The whole Austrian army is deploying on the other shore of the Alpone. We must take Arcole from them. Come on, come on, my friends, follow me.

(He rushes again on the bridge; grapeshot stops him as well as those who follow him.)

OFFICER

Impossible, General!

ALL

It's impossible!

BONAPARTE (arriving on horseback with officers)

Impossible? When the fate of Italy depends on you. Soldiers, once again an effort, and you will force Alvinczi to leave his fortified positions. Verona will be delivered, you will no longer have to fight an army twice our size, and tomorrow you will bring to Arcole a great victory.

(dismounting)

Look, are you still the victors of Lodi?

ALL

Yes, yes!

BONAPARTE (seizing the flag held by François)

Well, in that case, follow your general!

FRANÇOIS

Forward, my friends!

BONAPARTE

Forward!

ALL

Forward!

(The soldiers run to follow Bonaparte. The Austrians after a terrible discharge come to meet him. They are beaten on all sides)

THE FRENCH (yelling)

Victory! Victory!

(As Bonaparte reaches the middle of the bridge, the curtain falls.)

CURTAIN

SCENE V

Egypt, in the desert between Alexandria and Cairo.

Jérôme is flag-bearer and Saturnin, Sergeant. The Regiment arrives overwhelmed by weariness and heat. The soldiers wear their uniforms open and seem no longer able to march.

JÉRÔME

We ought to rest here for a few hours.

ANTOINE

It's all we can stand for today; no need to take the air for this.

JÉRÔME

To think that we are in Egypt.

ANTOINE

And in a pretty part of Egypt at that. The middle of the desert.

SATURNIN

François predicted correctly that our flag would make a tour of the world.

JÉRÔME

François had the honor of bearing it in Italy. The General-in Chief promoted him to Captain later, and now I am the one who carries our beloved standard.

SATURNIN

While waiting for it to be my turn. As for me, my friend, I have only one ambition. It's to die defending it.

JÉRÔME

Come on, will you, it's better to advance in rank, by planting it on the summit of some fortification as François did.

SATURNIN

That brave Captain. Here we are separated from him for the first time.

JÉRÔME

He went to carry an order from the Commanding General to Kleber. We'll meet him again beneath the walls of Cairo.

ANTOINE

Pardon, excuse my interrupting you, but now that the fog of morning is easing off, the Sun won't be slow to show itself, a Sun compared to which the dog days of France are but a moon in comparison.

SATURNIN

What do you expect us to do about it?

ANTOINE

If you've got tents it would be well to set them up in the next quarter of an hour.

JÉRÔME

It's not permitted for anyone to carry one with him.

ANTOINE

Then we'd better be careful! It's going to get hot. Hold on—it's rising. The desert is inundated with light. Hello, Sun!

JÉRÔME

Yes, a terrible heat.

ANTOINE (pointing to a young soldier and a piper)

And there are kids who have already suffered, I'm afraid that this fiery Sun may be fatal to them.

(to Piper)

Well! How are you feeling, kid?

PIPER

Bad, Papa Antoine. I am ashamed not to have more courage.

JÉRÔME

It's not courage you lack, kid, it's strength.

A YOUNG SOLDIER

You're right, lieutenant, it's strength we need.

PIPER

Ah, if I could breathe for a moment. Shade. But no, not one tree, not even a blade of grass.

YOUNG SOLDIER

Yes, at least if there was a little water. But all the pits, all the cisterns we have encountered are dry.

PIPER

It's all over. I can't take any more. I'm going to die here, I think, Papa Antoine!

ANTOINE

Come on, will you, kid. Is it possible after all, I told your mother I'd bring you back to her as a Junior Lieutenant, indeed, I have to bring you back as one.

PIPER

My head's on fire, Papa Antoine.

SATURNIN

Poor kid!

PIPER

It seems to me my blood's boiling in my head, and my mouth is dry. So bad that—I can't speak any more.

ANTOINE

Hell's bells! He's the son of my sister! If this kid dies to the devil with discipline. I'm going to shoot myself.

JÉRÔME

Shut up, wretch, shut up!

ANTOINE

And if I don't want to? Hold on, this expedition to Egypt. It's a diabolic ruse invented by the Directory so as to rid themselves of the brave Army of Italy.

FIRST SOLDIER

Perhaps well!

SATURNIN

You are mad!

ANTOINE

Yes, it's to kill us they sent us here.

JÉRÔME

Silence, I tell you.

ANTOINE

Come on, will you.

(Soldiers surround him and murmur with him)

FIRST SOLDIER

He's right.

ALL

Yes, yes, he's right!

JÉRÔME

Just one more day of courage and you will arrive under the walls of Cairo.

ANTOINE

And we'll get there so overwhelmed by fatigue, heat, and thirst, that the Bedouins will have nothing to do but watch us die.

ALL

Yes, it's true, yes, yes!

ANTOINE

And enough of this war with Egypt.

SATURNIN

Silence, here comes General Bonaparte.

ALL

Hey, yes, we'll tell him.

BONAPARTE (enters followed by two aides de camp)

Why did they prepare a tent for me? Who gave that order?

ANTOINE

What! He complains of that? Maybe it's too cool for him.

BONAPARTE

I don't want for me any other shelter than that my soldiers share.

ANTOINE

Ah!

JÉRÔME

What was it you said there, you?

ANTOINE

Me? I said—the fact is—that I thought it was hotter than this.

BONAPARTE

What's going on here? I heard shouts when I arrived.

(to Antoine)

Come on, reply.

ANTOINE

Damn! My General—it's—it's some sensitive to cold who complain of lack of heat, And then there's this child who's very ill. I don't know if it's from cold. But he's very ill, general.

BONAPARTE

Let them carry him. Give him this tent prepared for me.

ANTOINE

Holy cow, that's damn fine, really!

(He carries the Piper who passes in front of Bonaparte)

PIPER

You are saving my life, general.

ANTOINE

And I thank you in the name of his mother.

BONAPARTE (looking at Antoine's open uniform)

So, you are really hot.

ANTOINE (buttoning up)

On the contrary, General, I'm shivering.

BONAPARTE

So this regiment hasn't lost its energy?

ANTOINE

Never, never, General.

BONAPARTE

So much the better. The 18th isn't like you. It is allowing itself to be overcome without struggle, it murmurs, it even complains.

ANTOINE

Yuck! The 18th—wet chickens. Say there, comrades, the 18th complains of the heat! Are you hot, the rest of you?

ALL

No, no!

ANTOINE

It's not very hot, General. It's nice—very, very, nice.

BONAPARTE (aside)

Poor folks! They are trying to hide their suffering from me. And this suffering is already destroying their energy.

(The soldiers are overwhelmed again and allow themselves to fall at all sides.)

JÉRÔME

General, it seems that heaven heard you. Look down there.

BONAPARTE (forcefully)

The enemy! Ah, my star, my star! Stand up, comrades. Here's the enemy. It's victory coming to us.

ALL

The enemy! To arms! To arms!

BONAPARTE

Soldiers—reach that plateau. Form up in square battalions. Don't let the enemy cavalry join up. On all sides, let walls of iron vomit flame. Go!

ALL

Long live France!

(The Mamelukes, in magnificent costumes, commanded by Moussad-beg, arrive at a gallop. They try to encroach on the square battalions and are everywhere met by heavy fire. Forced to retreat they attack again and are again repulsed.

(They make a final effort. The most desperate try to overturn their horses on the battalions. Their attack becomes furious. The French are forced to retreat, but at this moment Desaix's division arrives. And Bonaparte causes a square battalion to open revealing a battalion which vomits death and spreads disorder among the Mamelukes who take flight.)

CURTAIN

SCENE VI

Cairo: a huge square.

AT RISE, numerous French soldiers appear.

ANTOINETTE

Well, here we are in this city of Cairo!

ANTOINE

And a little at our ease, to my mind.

ANTOINETTE

I still know folks who pretended we wouldn't get here.

(to ANTOINE)

Who was it said that?

ANTOINE (embarrassed)

Dunno!

ANTOINETTE

Well, who was it assured us that we'd only arrive too tired except to die beneath the walls of the city?

(to Antoine)

Who was it said stupidities like that?

ANTOINE

Dunno.

MOLINCHON

The fact is that for the French to arrive dying before the enemy, he'd have to be dead for several days.

ANTOINETTE

Bravo, Corporal Molinchon!

ALL

Bravo!

MOLINCHON

You are honoring my stripes, comrades!

ANTOINETTE

It's true, indeed, you are a corporal. But I would never have thought you would advance ahead of Citizen Boudinier.

BOUDINIER

Me neither, I never would have thought it.

MOLINCHON

Me neither. It's the result of chance. Indeed, I would have thought it would be Mr. Boudinier, who is so courageous, would be the one to make his stripes first.

BOUDINIER

The god of battles was dozing, he didn't see what was taking place, and Mr. Molinchon has blown my stripes.

ANTOINETTE

What! What do you mean, "blown"?

BOUDINIER

Ah, yes, actually. Let him deny it a bit.

ANTOINETTE

Why he captured a cannon all by himself.

BOUDINIER

Come on, he captured only by cowardice.

ALL

By cowardice!

BOUDINIER

Let him dare to deny it, too.

MOLINCHON

Well, it's true. Yes, I captured that cannon from fear.

ALL

From fear!

MOLINCHON

Purely from fear. I was so afraid he'd kill me with a cannon ball that I started running straight at it. Once I got there I found myself face to face with four artillery men who intended to kill me, so my fear increased, and bang! I shot one, and the others were coming straight at me, so my fear became frenetic, In my terror, I skewered one with my bayonet, I knocked down a third with my rifle butt, and the fourth took flight, and me, I seized the cannon. But I was really scared, I tell you.

ANTOINE

Meaning this lad doesn't suspect his courage!

BOUDINIER

And that's why I didn't get my stripes!

MOLINCHON

Excuse me, Mr. Boudinier, I'm quite ashamed of that.

ANTOINETTE

Ashamed of what?

MOLINCHON

I dare not picture my rank, I had the effect of a usurper. Will you forgive me for it, beautiful Antoinette?

BOUDINIER

Not at all. It's to my courage that her heart will belong.

MOLINCHON

Ah, no, no.

ANTOINETTE

This requires consideration.

BOUDINIER

Bah! I will be her lucky conqueror.

MOLINCHON

You, by God!

BOUDINIER

What's the matter with you?

MOLINCHON

Don't tell me you will be her happy conqueror.

BOUDINIER

And why not?

MOLINCHON

Don't say it, because coward though I am, and brave as you are—

BOUDINIER

Well? What then?

MOLINCHON

Nothing, except at the thought of that, I feel I'll put my saber in your torso.

BOUDINIER

You—

(trembling)

For—for goodness sakes!

MOLINCHON

No "for goodness sakes"—if you say it again I'll exterminate you.

BOUDINIER (trembling)

Why—why what's got into this poltroon?

MOLINCHON

Are you saying it? Are you saying It? Huh?

BOUDINIER

Well, no—no, I—

MOLINCHON (low)

I let myself get carried away. Pardon me, my brave Boudinier.

BOUDINIER

I pardon you.

ANTOINETTE

Do you hear the uproar they're making down there?

ANTOINE

The party's going to start.

ALL

The party?

ANTOINETTE

What party is that?

ANTOINE

The party of the Nile.

MOLINCHON

Because in Egypt we have abolished the Saints like in France. Today is the day of the Sacred Nile.

ALL (laughing)

Ha, ha, ha!

MOLINCHON (to Boudinier)

Did I say something stupid?

BOUDINIER

A little. Actually, you are as stupid as you are cowardly.

MOLINCHON (sighing)

I'm really stupid then.

ANTOINETE

And you are not less so near the beauties. You still brave the fire of Bellona, rather than that of love. Oh, God! If I were a man how I'd make you march toward the ladies. Two winks. After that three sighs. Josephine, I adore you. Since I love you, you must love me. One, two, carried off. And go, will you!

(she feigns twirling a mustache and takes on the manner of a trooper.)

BOUDINIER

Ah, she's a famous trooper, this Miss Antoinette.

ANTOINETTE

Just like Margoton, the Pearl of Vivandières.

ANTOINE

About whom they wrote a song. Sing it for us, Antoinette.

ALL

Yes, yes, the song.

ANTOINETTE

Well, attention—prepare yourselves for the refrain.

(sings)

She's Margoton the Vivandière
She fights like a soldier
Always the first at the battle,
Always the last to leave.
The first and last.
And thanks to her numerous exploits.
She acquired so much renown
That she would have had, I think, for lovers
All the soldiers of our army,
But she took no lover
Except the Regimental Flag.
Blah, blah blah (repeat)
You must drink
To her memory.
Blah, blah, blah (repeat)
Forward!
The drum is beating.

II.

Still, she placed few shackles
On the sweet transports she inspired
So each brave adored her.
She adored many braves (repeat)
But, each in turn, she deceives
The Sergeant for the Clarinette
The Colonel for the Drummer.
The Corporal for the Trumpet.
She loved with fidelity
Only the regimental flag.
Blah, blah, blah, etc.

III.

It's to refresh victory,
That all her springtime passed.
Then a cannon ball got her.
Still she gave some drinks (repeat)
That day the enemy fled.
And not thinking of her suffering
As she fell, she yelled:
Long live France!
Then they buried her sacredly
In the regimental flag.
Blah, blah, blah
You must drink ,etc.

ANTOINE

The great religious ceremony is going to begin.

MOLINCHON

Why, what ceremony?

ANTOINE

Of the Nile, I told you. They are going to open the dikes, and this gentleman's going to make his bed in the field. It's like this every year. And they've been celebrating it 22,000 years in this country.

ALL

Twenty-two thousand years!

ANTOINE

And today, the Commanding General wants to be present in person, Ah, hold on, here's the procession.

ANTOINETTE

Come on, come on, make room for the darkies. (Moors)

(Enter Bonaparte and his suite)

ALL

The General!

(The Sheik arrives followed by his court and bows before Bonaparte)

SHEIK

May Great Allah make the Army of Occidental Braves and Sultan Khebir prosper.

BONAPARTE

People of Egypt for too long the Beys who govern you have insulted the French Nation. For too long this bunch of slaves, purchased in the Caucasus and Georgia tyrannized over the most beautiful part of the world. God, on whom all depend has ordered their empire overthrown, and we came to free you.

SHEIK

Glory to Sultan Khebir!

ALL

Glory to him! Glory to him!

BONAPARTE

France thanks you through my voice. I am going to bring to old Cairo the pledge of peace. Don't let the party be interrupted!

(Bonaparte moves away with his suite.)

WOLF (aside)

Now comes the manifesto that the Sublime Porte promised us, and these here won't hesitate.

SHEIK

What are the people saying?

WOLF

They are waiting for the signal to revolt.

SHEIK

Speak in my name to the principal chiefs. The Sun won't set before I've given the signal.

WOLF

They are prepared. They've sworn to exterminate the French to the last man.

(The ceremony of the Nile begins)

First, a marriage takes place. They are bringing on a shield the Statue of the Bride of the Nile.

SHEIK

Sons of Mohammet, this statue represents the bride of the Nile, according to customs. I cast this image into the waters of the Sacred River, and I accomplish the union which is the augery of the fertility of our fields, and the prosperity of the children of Egypt.

Blessed be this marriage.

ALL

Blessed be it!

SHEIK

Break the dikes!

VOICES (far off, becoming more distant)

Break the dikes! Break the dikes!

(Fanfares are heard as well as voices, all become more distant)

(A BALLET)

(After the first part of the ballet, he goes from one group to another to incite hatred of the French. A horseman arrives with a parchment.)

WOLF

The Manifesto, perhaps!

(The horseman gives the Sheik a parchment, bows and moves away.)

SHEIK (to those around him)

From the Commander of Believers—Listen, listen. "The French are an obstinate nation of infidels!"

ALL

Yes, yes!

SHEIK

"O you, worshippers of a single God, march to battle, and as the dust disperses the wind, there will remain no vestige of the infidels, for the promise of God is formal—the bad guys will perish. Glory to the Lord of Worlds."

ALL

Glory to the Lord of Worlds.

WOLF

And death to the French.

ALL

And death to the French!

WOLF (opening a door to a palace)

Hold on, here are the weapons.

(shouts off)

Do you hear? This firman, read in every town has awakened the rage of believers, their shouts of hate and death, respond to your screams! To arms! To arms!

ALL

To arms!

(they distribute weapons)

FRANÇOIS (carrying the flag)

This way, comrades, this way! From the height of this terrace a signal can be seen from a distance. The revolt is everywhere. Our friends, our brothers, spread through the city and in the fields are going to be butchered in isolation; it's necessary to rally them so they can defend themselves. A signal known by all.

(he raises the flag and climbs the steps of a palace.)

From this height I will make this standard flutter so they can see it, so they'll rush and join us here! I will carry it until death strikes me. If I fall, replace me until the last one of you.

ALL

Yes, yes!

(They surround François, who waves the flag)

WOLF (returning with armed Egyptians)

François—the flag—it's a signal. Fire on them.

(The Egyptians fire; The French return the fire, but four fall.)

FRANÇOIS

Wounded! Never mind. Close your ranks, my friends, close your ranks.

WOLF (to his Egyptians)

Stop! I want to see him stagger and bow before me. I want to see his flag fallen in the dust.

FRANÇOIS

Before him, never!

WOLF (shooting at François and wounding him again)

Fire!

(Several Egyptians fire, too. Two more French fall.)

FRANÇOIS (wounded)

Courage, comrades. Each minute we gain can save fifty of our brothers. They've seen the flag. There they are! There they are! Fire!

(They step forward. Wolf and the others fire and he is wounded again. François staggers, and holds the flag straight by leaning on the stalk.)

WOLF

Keep it up!

(François falls)

I told you I would force you to abandon it.

FRANÇOIS

No: so long as a breath of life remains to me, it will not fall!

(The Egyptians enter en masse.)

WOLF

We'll see about that.

(Wolf rushes François, saber in hand; At the same moment Saturnin rushes between them, aided by Jérôme. The Egyptians arrive in great numbers. The battle begins when Bonaparte arrives on horseback.)

BONAPARTE

Stop! My artillery surrounds you, ready to wipe you out. Put down your weapons and I will pardon you.

WOLF

No! We don't ask for mercy; we won't lay down our arms.

ALL THE EGYPTIANS

No! No!

BONARPARTE

Grenadiers, forward!

(The grenadiers enter and drive the Egyptians before them.)

CURTAIN

SCENE VII

Vienna: a public square.

NINA

Well, what news of the war?

GERTRUDE

What news? Eh, my God, always the same. When they tell us we've won battles, that our husbands behaved like heroes, that the French are in full retreat, the enemy keeps advancing.

WOMEN

It's true, it's true!

BOUDINIER

Bah! You know nothing of strategy.

GERTRUDE

Big word, that's all. The French beat us at Ulm.

BOUDINIER

Because they outnumbered us, but since then—

GERTRUDE

Since then they beat the Russians. The Austrians joined them, and then, May God will it that the French are beaten as they were until now, because after such a defeat they are surrounding Vienna.

ALL

Ah!

NINA (to Boudinier)

What do you say to that?

BOUDINIER

She knows nothing of strategy.

(They move away. Saturnin enters with his arm in a scarf. Wolf wears an Austrian uniform.)

WOLF

Well, my poor Saturnin, why are you so sad, so overwhelmed?

SATURNIN

Why? Because instead of being here in Vienna, with the triumphant French army—

WOLF

You're a prisoner here.

SATURNIN

Prisoner! If, at least, I was alone.

WOLF

Yes, the flag is with you as well.

SATURNIN (sorrowfully)

The flag!

WOLF

The wound you received made you lose consciousness, but you clung to your standard so energetically, pressed against your breast, that to take one it was necessary to take both of you.

SATURNIN

And to think that the French army is only a few leagues from here.

WOLF

Between Vienna and that army is the Danube. On this side of the river there's numerous artillery protecting the passage. The wooden bridge which serves to communicate from one shore to the other will be blown up as soon as the French show themselves. Before they are capable of constructing another, the Russian Army and the Austrian Armies will have time to join and crush their enemies.

SATURNIN

Yes, a new battle is shaping up and I won't be there. Oh, why am I not dead?

WOLF

Don't despair like that; is your fate here so terrible? In memory of our former acquaintance I've obtained for you permission to walk the streets. You're a prisoner on parole. Free to go where you like.

SATURNIN

Yes, but you accompany me everywhere.

WOLF

Right. I bother you, and I know why.

SATURNIN

You know!

WOLF

You received a letter this morning.

SATURNIN (with emotion)

A letter.

WOLF (watching him)

A love letter, I am certain.

SATURNIN (with constraint)

Yes, a love letter. Yes, yes, that's it.

WOLF (aside)

He's upset.

(aloud)

Ah, our beautiful Viennese take a touching interest in prisoners who are young and handsome. And my presence might annoy you a bit.

SATURNIN

I admit it.

WOLF (aside)

Come on! There's a mystery here that I'll unravel.

(aloud)

Well, Mr. Saturnin, I do not include you in the mortal hate that I bear to one of your two friends, and you are free to seek the consolations of your captivity.

SATURNIN

Thanks, Mr. Wolf. I'd like to be able to thank you for what you've done for me.

WOLF

Nothing could be easier. I left France a long while ago. Tell me what's become of—

SATURNIN

Of whom? The three young embroiderers?

WOLF

Yes, speak.

SATURNIN

A few months ago during the peace of 1804, when the Empire had just been decreed, when they were going to distribute new flags to the Army, we who wanted to keep ours—we employed a stratagem.

WOLF

What do you mean?

SATURNIN

François molded and chiseled the Eagle which was to replace the Fer-de-Lance, and to change the inscription we ran to the shop of the pretty embroiderers. There were only two left. Louise and Jeanne. They waited for us, the brave girls, a few days later, they were calling themselves Madame Jérôme and Madame Saturnin.

WOLF

And Marie? Marie?

SATURNIN

The Emperor had just reopened the gates of France to the Émigrés. Mr. De Marsilly returned to his country, and didn't believe he was lowering himself by granting the hand of his daughter to Commandant Beaudoin.

WOLF

His wife! She's his wife?

(aside)

Come on. All I will live for now is to satisfy my hate.

SATURNIN

But there's still someone of whom you doubtless have to ask me news.

WOLF

Of whom are you speaking?

SATURNIN

Of your mother.

WOLF

Oh, my mother! No.— Well, yes, speak to me of her. She curses me, right?

SATURNIN

She weeps for your death.

WOLF

My death! Why, she believes then—

SATURNIN

She knows that you've renounced your country, that you fight under the flag of an enemy of France, and, as I told you, she weeps over your death.

WOLF (aside)

Oh, wretch, wretch that I am.

(aloud)

François, it's on you that I'll avenge myself! And, if my suspicions don't deceive me, that will be soon.

(he moves away)

SATURNIN (watching him leave)

Finally! He made me trouble! He knows I received a letter which gave me a meeting here. Luckily, he's on the wrong scent. But who are the friends that must come. This handwriting that I think I recognize— No, it's impossible.

(Jérôme and François appear dressed as German peasants. They come and shake hands with Saturnin.)

FRANÇOIS

Saturnin, my friend.

SATURNIN

You here!

FRANÇOIS

Yes, we pursued those who carried you off, wrapped in our flag that we swore to die for or snatch you both from their hands, that night you were overtaken, separated from our camp by enemy lines.

SATURNIN

Why, you are lost!

JÉRÔME

Who knows? We've already been able to procure these clothes.

SATURNIN

Then profit by it and attempt to return to the French camp.

FRANÇOIS

Return—without bringing the flag! Is it possible? Ah, if you had seen with what fury our soldiers rushed in pursuit of those who carried it away, with what heroism they braved death, if you had heard their shouts of despair and rage! Grape shot decimated them, they kept coming. They fell by the hundreds, and those who were expiring raised themselves up, stretching their hands towards us, shouting, "My friends, save, save the flag!"

SATURNIN

My brave comrades—

FRANÇOIS

And you want us to return without it? It's impossible! Our honor is imprisoned here, with the flag, and I will return only with it at the head of my regiment.

SATURNIN

You are right, my friends, in your place I would act as you are doing.

(Molinchon and Boudinier enter disguised as Tyrolean peasants, singing)

SATURNIN (to François)

Silence!

MOLINCHON (approaching, in a German accent)

Don't forget the little singer, if you please.

BOUDINIER

The little singer, my good gentlemen.

MOLINCHON

The little zinger.

(resumes, militarily)

My commandant.

FRANÇOIS

What do I see? Why, it's—

JÉRÔME

Molinchon.

MOLINCHON

And the brave Boudinier.

BOUDINIER

All in one piece, yes, my commandant.

FRANÇOIS

But how is it that—?

MOLINCHON

Ah, that's the thing! When I saw you hadn't returned to camp, neither you, nor the flag, I said to myself, "They're all in Vienna. You must go there, Molinchon." I asked permission from the General for the two of us. I borrowed the clothes we are wearing, me and Boudinier, from peasants, and like some villagers at a party we crossed through the two camps singing, Ja did ah.

FRANÇOIS

Ah. You had the same thought we had, That's fine. And courage hasn't failed you.

MOLINCHON

Oh! Courage! Boudinier has enough for both of us.

BOUDINIER

Yes, yes. I had it.

MOLINCHON

Only when he found himself here, the brave Boudinier had such a comical and pale look of surprise on his face that I laughed like a crazy little girl.

JÉRÔME

Ah, Boudinier didn't know he was coming to Vienna.

BOUDINIER

It's true, Captain, that—I didn't imagine—completely—that it was—

MOLINCHON

A bunch, my commandant, a whole bunch of information.

BOUDINIER

Yes, women, pretty women. They are not shy or stuck up.

FRANÇOIS

And you discovered?

MOLINCHON

In what place the flag is locked up.

FRANÇOIS

Fine, fine, my friends.

SATURNIN

And then?

MOLINCHON

And then? We've found the means of seizing it.

WOLF (aside)

I wasn't mistaken. Let's listen.

FRANÇOIS

Finally.

MOLINCHON

Finally, the dear flag is at Fort Saint André.

ALL

At Fort Saint André.

BOUDINIER

Saint André.

MOLINCHON

It's there. We saw it there.

WOLF (aside)

Fine!

MOLINCHON

It's guarded, because of the needs of the war, only by some invalids and three or four vigorous and well-armed men could easily deal with the old men who remain at the fort.

FRANÇOIS

We will take charge of that, Jérôme and I.

JÉRÔME

But weapons—?

BOUDINIER

Here are some pocket clarinets.

(pulling some pistols from beneath his robe)

MOLINCHON

And here are their sisters.

FRANÇOIS (taking two pistols)

At Fort Saint André. We'll be there in a quarter of an hour.

WOLF (aside)

I'll be there before you, François.

(Wolf leaves.)

JÉRÔME

Let's go.

SATURNIN

Yes, let's go!

MOLINCHON

One moment, I still have a word to say.

JÉRÔME

Speak.

MOLINCHON

First of all, the Lieutenant, seen in his uniform, cannot be part of it.

FRANÇOIS

It's true.

MOLINCHON

After that, you will leave for Saint André, right?

JÉRÔME and FRANÇOIS

Yes, yes.

MOLINCHON

You get there, you ask to see the flag, no?

FRANÇOIS

No question.

MOLINCHON

They will give you an escort, and instead of leading you to the flag, they'll take you to the Guard Room, where that swine of a Mr. Wolf will be waiting for you with twenty or thirty men, and you'll be shot like spies.

SATURNIN and JÉRÔME

What do you mean?

FRANÇOIS

What's it signify?

MOLINCHON

It signifies, my commandant, that the brigand was there, spying on us, and I duped him, that's all!

ALL

Wolf!

BOUDINIER

Kill the Kaiserlick!

MOLINCHON and BOUDINIER (dancing)

La-di dah, la did ah.

FRANÇOIS

What, the wretch—?

MOLINCHON

I sent him to Saint-André, and it's there, at the large fort, that our dear flag is prisoner.

FRANÇOIS

Ah, it will soon be free. Once we get it in our hands, we will cut the stalk, we will hide the eagle and the flag under our clothes, and, at peril of our lives we will cross the enemy lines. Let's go. And may God protect us!

JÉRÔME

Let's go!

MOLINCHON

Well— And what about us?

BOUDINIER

And what about us?

FRANÇOIS

So be it. Come, come.

MOLINCHON (pulling Boudinier)

Come on.

BOUDINIER

What a strange picnic!

(They leave.)

SATURNIN

May they succeed. Let them hurry, especially, because once he gets to Saint André, that wretch Wolf will realize he's been tricked; he'll run with all his men where the flag is really to be found— And then all will be lost. Oh, I don't want to abandon them. I'm going to go.

(noise of clocks and acclamations)

What's all that?

(Boudinier and men of the people enter in confusion.)

(To Boudinier.)

What's wrong?

BOUDINIER

The French army is entering Vienna.

SATURNIN

The French Army? Is it really possible? The bridge that had to be blown up? The artillery that was supposed to stop us?

BOUDINIER

Those French devils used trickery and audacity. Two superior officers, two generals crossed the bridge. They seized the artillery officer who was going to blow it up. Upstarts on the other shore addressed themselves to the cannoneers, demanded to speak to the general who commands in the city, and while they spoke, a column of grenadiers, hidden by large trees near the river and wooded islands, rushed out suddenly, seized our cannons, and disarmed our artillery.

SATURNIN

And the French Army, you say?

BOUDINIER

The French army is entering Vienna.

SHOUTS

They are here! They are here!

(noise of clocks and cannons. The Army enters, Napoleon in its midst.)

NAPOLEON

Soldiers, the people of Vienna, according to the expression of the deputations from the faubourgs, forsaken and abandoned, will be the object of your cares. I am taking the inhabitants under my special protection.

ALL

Long live the Emperor!

NAPOLEON

Soldiers of the 12th, I witnessed your courage during the battle, your heroic efforts to regain the flag that an enemy twenty times more numerous was able to snatch from your hands. That flag will be returned to you.

FRANÇOIS

Here it is, Sire, here it is!

(carrying the flag)

ALL THE SOLDIERS

The flag! The flag!

(They rush to François. Each wants to see it again, to touch it; some kneel to embrace it.)

NAPOLEON

Commandant Beaudoin.

FRANÇOIS

Sire, if your army hadn't entered Vienna victorious today, tomorrow I would have brought this flag to Your Majesty, or I would have died attempting to free it.

NAPOLEON

That's fine. Approach, Colonel.

ALL

Colonel.

FRANÇOIS

Ah, Sire,

NAPOLEON

Soldiers, I once again want to honor the bravery of each of you.

(removing his cross which he attaches to the flag)

Flag of the 12th, in the name of France, which has adopted your colors, in the name of whose honor you are the sign, in the name of the father-land whose defenders you lead, I decorate you with the Cross of The Brave.

ALL

Long live the Emperor! Long live the Emperor!

CURTAIN

SCENE VIII

Moscow. A cabin erected on Mount Salud in the neighborhood of Moscow. Large doors and windows which are open allowing the golden domes and golden bells of Moscow to be seen.

SATURNIN

Moscow, Moscow. The holy city that we can see from here.

JÉRÔME

Yes, there are its domes, its golden bells, which shine in the Sun. And all that is ours.

SATURNIN

Ah! How many miracles accomplished since the beginning of the Empire! How many victories at which our glorious flag was present! Ulm, Austerlitz, Jena, Friedland.

JÉRÔME

Eckmuhl, Wagram, and last but not least, Smolensk and Moscow.

SATURNIN

We planted it in Berlin, in Madrid, in Vienna. And tomorrow it will triumphantly enter Moscow.

JÉRÔME

Yes, our division under the orders of Marshall Ney, of the Prince of Moscow, has encamped here today again with the wounded, three leagues from the city.

SATURNIN

And Jeanne, Marie, and Louise are here lavishing their cares on the unfortunate victims of the war.

JÉRÔME

Ah, they've got excellent hearts. After becoming our wives they no longer want to leave us, they followed the Army even unto Russia. They are the Providence of the sick and wounded.

(Louise and Marie support Antoine, who's wounded in the leg; Molinchon, wounded in the shoulder, leans on Jeanne's arm.)

MARIE

Come on, courage, lean on us.

ANTOINE

How kind you are, ladies!

JEANNE (to Molinchon)

Lean on us, will you, Sergeant-Major.

MOLINCHON

Excuse, me Madame. It's cause I don't dare.

JEANNE

You don't dare?

ANTOINE

Bah! Bah! He imagines that, the Sergeant. He still thinks he'd never dare do anything, and he's a devil that nothing stops.

MOLINCHON

Antoine!

SATURNIN

Excellent hearts!

JÉRÔME

Ah, you are nice women, all three of you!

LOUISE

Instead of heaping compliments on us, tell your soldiers to obey us a bit.

JÉRÔME

They will obey you, Madame, I insist on it.

LOUISE

Right.

JEANNE

You hear?

ANTOINE

We'll obey.

MOLINCHON

We'll obey.

BOUDINIER (bringing in two cups of bouillon; he's dressed as a nurse)

Here's bouillon to strengthen the wounded.

JÉRÔME

Why! I recognize this lad! One of my old soldiers.

BOUDINIER

Yes, Captain.

MOLINCHON

And a brave one.

JÉRÔME

Brave. In that case why'd he pass into the Nurse Corps?

BOUDINIER

I'm going to tell you. I was of disproportionate courage. I dare to say it.

MOLINCHON

Ah, indeed. I attest to it.

ANTOINE

Thanks.

BOUDINIER

But I ever had luck in the game of war.

ALL

Luck?

BOUDINIER

There's a prodigious amount of luck in grades, in glorious rewards. I'm not saying that about you, Sergeant-Major. I don't wish to wither your laurels.

MOLINCHON

Thanks, Mr. Boudinier.

BOUDINIER

But seeing that fate was blind in my regard, I went into nursing and I've become a mother for the wounded.

ALL (laughing)

A mother.

BOUDINIER

I dare to say it.

MOLINCHON

A man who had so much courage. What a shame he never got a place.

ANTOINE

Let me be! You're the only one who ever saw his courage.

SATURNIN

But where the devil is François?

JÉRÔME

The Emperor ordered that a party of ambulances be transported to Moscow. The Colonel followed with a battalion to escort them.

MARIE

Yes, a great number of wounded have left already. That's why our good Madame Wolf is no longer with us. She's accompanying them, too.

JÉRÔME

Madame Wolf. Another one who didn't want to separate from

us.

SATURNIN

Still, she has neither friend nor relative to follow.

JEANNE

She said she had a son she had to forget.

LOUISE

And she cares for the poor wounded with admirable courage.

MARIE

It seems that by the strength of devotion to her country she wants to cause her son's treason to be forgotten, and she's seeking absolution for giving him life.

JEANNE

Unhappy mother.

A SOLDIER (entering)

Marshall Ney.

NEY

The rest of the wounded will be transported to Moscow no later than tomorrow.

ANTOINE

Marshall, the peasants who must furnish wagons are here. They are waiting for you orders.

NEY

Show them in.

WOLF

The Marshall has called for us?

NEY

Let the means of transport be ready for tomorrow. You will be generously paid. It's the Emperor's order.

WOLF

The Emperor? Of the French?

NEY

And who else commands in Moscow? Ah, I know that General Kutuzov proclaims himself conqueror of our army.

ALL

Kutuzov!

NEY

He's taken a thousand prisoners, among them are the King of Naples, the Prince-Viceroy, the Prince d'Eckmuhl, and I actually don't know if Mr. Kutuzov hasn't killed me with his own hands.

JÉRÔME

That was a strange bulletin.

NEY

And we've been taken with the others to Saint Petersburg.

WOLF (with irony)

To Saint Petersburg?

NEY

Do you doubt it?

WOLF

It's a long way from here!

NEY

It was a long way from Paris to Moscow and we got here.

WOLF

Yes, you came in Autumn.

NEY

And despite Kutuzov.

WOLF

There's another general who hasn't yet given battle. General Winter.

ALL

General Winter!

NEY

Will winter be harder for us than for the Russians? Won't we move to Saint Petersburg?

WOLF

And if Saint Petersburg is burned?

NEY

Come on, they wouldn't dare do that!

WOLF

And why wouldn't they burn Saint Petersburg as well as Moscow?

NEY

Such an act of barbarism! They wouldn't dare, I tell you!

(bells ring in the distance)

WOLF

They wouldn't dare?

(going to open the door)

Well—hold on. Look.

ALL

Ah!

(They see Moscow enveloped in flames)

NEY

Why then it's a war with savages we are fighting.

WOLF

Perhaps.

NEY

This arson is perhaps a signal for revolt, the signal for the return of Kutuzov and other corps of the Russian army. and the Emperor is down there with only two divisions.

ALL

The Emperor.

NEY

Let's leave, my friends, let's leave. You, ladies, join the wounded.

(To Wolf and his peasants)

Wait for me to issue new orders before putting yourselves en route.

WOLF

We will wait.

(Ney and the other soldiers leave. Wolf gestures. All the peasants surround him while the women say their goodbyes to their husbands.)

As soon as they are far away surround this house, and when I fire this pistol, rush in followed by your brothers and be ready to execute my orders.

PEASANT

We are ready.

WOLF

Go.

(The peasants leave. Wolf remains alone with the women.)

MARIE

The ravages of the fire are spreading further and further.

LOUISE

Yes. See, down there. Yet another section is burning.

JEANNE

The sight of this horrible disaster makes me ill.

MARIE

It shakes my heart. It seems to presage some great misfortune.

WOLF

A great misfortune? You are not mistaken, Madame.

MARIE

What do you mean?

WOLF

I ought not—

MARIE

Explain yourself.

WOLF

Hold on, you interest me. Madame, I've seen you at the bedside of the sick, caring without distinction for your compatriots and those of my nation. That profoundly touched me, and perhaps, I can render you an important service.

MARIE

Hasten, I'm listening.

LOUISE and JEANNE

Yes, yes, speak.

WOLF

It's a question of a great secret. Probably, I'm risking my life in revealing it, and only before a single one of you. (pointing to Marie) before Madame that I can convince myself to speak.

MARIE

Jeanne, Louise, distance yourselves.

JEANNE

But—

MARIE

Possibly, it's a question of our safety, of the safety of the unfortunates who are here. Leave me alone, leave me alone. I insist on it, I beg you.

(as she leads them to the door, Wolf rids himself of his beard and his Russian hat.)

MARIE (returning)

Now you can speak.

WOLF

And I will speak, Marie.

MARIE

You! It's you!

WOLF

Myself.

MARIE

Here!

WOLF

What's so strange in that? Doesn't there exist in France a party which dreams of returning to the way things used to be? That party covers each country in Europe with its envoys: they spread through Italy, Spain, Prussia, Austria. Their number had nothing which bothers; it's not the party that pays.

MARIE

You sacrifice yourself for this party?

WOLF

The party thinks it is using me, I'm the one who's using it. What do I care about the cause that they defend? I know only one, that of my hate for François who you've never ceased to prefer to me, that of my love which absence hasn't strangled.

MARIE

Your love?

WOLF

Listen carefully to me, Marie. I've taken two solemn, terrible, irrevocable oaths. I've sworn the ruin of my rival and that you will be mine.

MARIE

As for me, sir, I've taken only one oath; that of living and dying for my husband.

WOLF

As for him, this François that I abhor! You'll never see him again.

MARIE

What will prevent me?

WOLF

I will. I've only to say one word, give one signal for a hundred arms to come to my aid. Ah, your friends have ordered the preparation of horses, carriages. I've faithfully executed their orders. A carriage is there which awaits us, and relays prepared in advance will soon carry us to the other side of Russia. Come on, Madame, come on. Prepare to follow me.

MARIE

Follow you! Why, I still have defenders here that I can call to my aid.

WOLF

Do it! But remember my words, there are women and wounded here. I'll give the signal for their death if your defenders cross the sill of this door.

MARIE

The signal for their death!

WOLF

Two hundred men await the noise of this weapon to present

themselves here. Two hundred men very thirsty for vengeance, and ready to shed blood—that blood will fall on your head.

MARIE

My God! What to do? What will happen?

WOLF

Will you force me to give the signal?

(Louise and Jeanne enter.)

LOUISE

Give it, sir!

JEANNE

Give it, we are ready to die.

MARIE (running to them)

Ah!

WOLF (rushing to the door, pistol in hand)

Well, since that's what you want!

(opening the door to come face to face with Madame Wolf, who strides towards him, pale and cold, forcing him to recoil)

Ma!

(heavy, thick voice)

She! She!

MADAME WOLF

Why don't you shoot? Is it a target worthy of you that you lack?

Hang on!

(she presents her breast)

Strike! Come on, don't tremble. Don't be afraid. I am only a woman.

WOLF

Mother! Mother!

(Wolf lets his pistol fall)

MADAME WOLF (picking it up)

Ah, you were going to add a new shame to all your past shames, one more crime to all your past crimes; you were going to call your accomplices to butcher women and wounded; that's truly the last degree of treason, isn't it? The measure is complete. I'm the one who'll give the signal they are waiting for. But you won't be here anymore, wretch, to dictate your infamous orders.

WOLF

What do you mean?

MADAME WOLF

On your knees.

WOLF

No.

MADAME WOLF

Unnatural son. On your knees, perjured citizen, traitor to your country, on your knees, Murderer! Parricide! On your knees! On your knees! You are going to die.

WOLF

It's impossible. You won't kill your son.

MADAME WOLF

My son. Look at your outfit. Am I the mother of a Russian? You have two mothers, France and me! You repudiated France, I am repudiating you in my turn.

MARIE

Curse him, kick him out, Madame. But don't kill him. In the name of his father, don't kill him.

MADAME WOLF

In the name of his father, you say? But his father was a soldier killed by an enemy bullet, and he, the wretch! He's spent so much time with the enemies of France that he may have shaken the hand that killed his father.

WOLF

Shut up, mother, you're driving me crazy.

MADAME WOLF

Ah, you see plainly I am right to call you parricide, you see plainly I'm right to want you to die.

WOLF

Well, yes, yes, kill me, kill me, mother—but stop talking to me like this.

(weeping)

I prefer to die. I prefer to die.

MADAME WOLF

I've seen you weep, wretch. I can't do it anymore. I can't do it anymore.

(she let's her arm fall that's holding the pistol.)

WOLF (grasping her hand and adroitly taking the pistol)

Mother! Mother!

(aside)

Ah!

(going to open the door)

MADAME WOLF

Where are you going?

WOLF

I haven't stopped loving you, mother, but I haven't stopped hating the man who stole Marie's heart from me. The day of vengeance has come, and I'm avenging myself.

(he fires the pistol)

MADAME WOLF (raising her head and letting out a scream of horror)

Aie!

WOLF

Seize these wounded and these women. I'll meet you in Kaluga.

PEASANTS

In Kaluga.

ANTOINE

What's the matter?

WOLF

You are our prisoners.

ALL

Prisoners!

WOLF

Come on, let's go. As for you, Marie, you won't leave me.

(trying to take her in his arms)

MARIE (struggling)

Leave me alone! Leave me alone!

ANTOINE

Forward, my friends! Let's protect the Colonel's wife.

MOLINCHON

Yes, forward! So much the worse!

WOLF

If you take a step, it's all over for you. Let's go.

(trying to drag Marie)

MARIE

No, no, I'd sooner die.

(general reaction. Clarions can be Heard outside.)

WOLF

What's that?

ANTOINE

The French!

ALL

The French!

ANTOINE (forcefully)

It's the escort the Marshal is sending with the wounded.

MARIE

Ah!

FRANÇOIS (rushing in and snatching her from Wolf's arms)

Wretch! Him! Wolf! Wolf!

WOLF

François!

FRANÇOIS

This is the last with which you will besmirch yourself, Frédéric Wolf. Ah, you said it, it was a mortal hate, a war without pity as without honor, and you ought not, in your eyes, to recoil from any trap, before any treachery, no matter how cowardly and shameful they might be.

WOLF (ironic)

Ah, you are noble and generous enemies, you insult the vanquished.

FRANÇOIS

Is he who traffics with his conscience, and sell his sword worthy of respect? Can he speak honestly, he who rejects his nation, who fights against his country, and who dishonors the name of his father?

WOLF (forcefully)

Enough! We planned to carry off your wounded and your women. Why are you waiting to pronounce our sentence?

FRANÇOIS

Seize them and let them be shot within the hour.

MARIE (frightened)

All!

MADAME WOLF

My God, his punishment is just, but after his punishment—grant him your pardon from on high!

MARIE (taking François by the hand and pointing to Madame Wolf.)

François!

FRANÇOIS

Oh—she's here. Poor woman, poor mother.

MARIE

She took care of me, she risked her life for me, can you before her, order her son's death?

FRANÇOIS (after a pause, going to Wolf)

Bless her, the one who weeps and prays for you. I have pity for her sorrow, for her tears. Get out of here. I am granting you mercy.

WOLF

What are you saying? You are granting me mercy? Come off it, it's impossible.

FRANÇOIS

It's not for you, I tell you, it's for her.

WOLF

Your pity is an insult, I don't want it.

MARIE

What's he saying?

WOLF

François Beaudoin, trust me, have me killed, because if I find you again one day, I feel I won't spare you.

FRANÇOIS

Your mother spared Marie; I'm giving you mercy.

WOLF

Marie? Why the sole thought of my life will be to tear her from you, as I would have done just now. If I don't die, I swear she will belong to me. Have me killed, I tell you.

FRANÇOIS (beside himself)

Wretch!

MARIE

François!

(she again points to Madame Wolf)

François!

MADAME WOLF

My God! At least let him repent.

(François goes to Madame Wolf, shakes her hand then goes back to the soldiers)

FRANÇOIS

Take the prisoners away.

(He approaches Wolf, supporting Madame Wolf)

MADAME WOLF

Take me away, take me away! What am I doing here since I no longer have a son?

FRANÇOIS

You know quite well you still have one. In the past, didn't I swear to be your son?

WOLF

That name to her! Don't call her mother. I don't want that

FRANÇOIS

You don't want me to be her son? So as to keep the right to murder me? Well, keep that right. When fate places us in each other's presence, kill me if you can, and I will have vengeance in advance of your crime. Come, mother.

(all leave except Wolf)

WOLF (alone)

Spared, saved by him. But what's taking place in the heart of that man? We will see each other again, François, we will see each other again.

(he leaves.)

CURTAIN

SCENE IX

The retreat from Moscow: a desert covered with snow.

Antoine, Boudinier, Molinchon, Antoinette, and soldiers enter dressed in tatters. Their worn-out shoes are replaced with improvised straw.

AT RISE, they fire a few shots at the unseen enemy.

ANTOINE

The humming birds flew off.

ANTOINETTE

They outnumber us three to one; they've gone for reinforcements!

MOLINCHON

It's really six to one!

BOUDINIER

There—I counted them. Sixty men, and there are twenty of us.

MOLINCHON

Sixty men, so be it, sixty horses—that makes a hundred twenty.

BOUDINIER

Horses—do horses fight?

MOLINCHON

No, but they eat, that's not to be scorned.

ALL

Oh, no, no.

ANTOINE

What a campaign! We mustn't sugar the pill. We are not at the end of it.

ANTOINETTE

Fifteen hundred of us left Moscow, and here's what's left.

MOLINCHON

It's still more than you can feed, vivandiére.

ANTOINETTE

Hell, gang, I shared all that I had, and when the canteen became empty it broke my heart to see all these brave soldiers falling around me without my being able to give them a drop of brandy or a crust of bread.

BOUDINIER

I haven't eaten in three day, that's rough.

MOLINCHON

As for me, my brain's so distracted that I no longer know what day I ate. Ah, yes, my last meal was in the ruins of the village of Strogoff, pheasant with cabbage. Actually, there wasn't any pheasant, but the cabbage was deliciously good.

ANTOINE

The village of Strogoff. That's where we became separated from our poor Colonel.

BOUDINIER

And our two friends.

ANTOINETTE

And my former employer.

ANTOINE

Heaven is our witness that it's those who ordered us to continue our route and try to reach Smolensk— And indeed, he failed to obey.

ANTOINETTE

And what a spectacle on the route! Men numbed and frozen succumbing in sleep that brought death! Others dying of fatigue and hunger, disorder everywhere. No discipline. Each thinks for himself. They spread out in all directions to search for bread.

BOUDINIER

They met only Cossacks.

MOLINCHON

And that is not edible. It's very hard.

ANTOINE

Come on, children, we must continue on our way. Let no one stop. You know, rest, sleep is death. En route!

ALL (sadly)

En route!

(They move away. Soon the Cossacks enter, observing them and following them. Then they move away in their turn. The stage remains empty. The wind blows forcefully, and the snow falls in large flakes.)

(François, Jérôme, and Saturnin enter, barely able to walk. Their clothes are in tatters.)

SATURNIN

The Cossacks are moving away. Let's stop for a moment.

FRANÇOIS

Yes, because strength abandons me. I don't know how to continue.

JÉRÔME

Still, a little courage, my friends. Yet one more supreme effort. Salvation may be but a few steps off.

FRANÇOIS

Salvation! There's no more for us, alas! Look at what surrounds us. Immense plains covered with snow.

SATURNIN

Desert everywhere!

FRANÇOIS

Death everywhere. What a shocking climate. It's not the enemy who is vanquishing us. We are all dying of hunger and cold.

SATURNIN

And that's the fate that awaits us.

FRANÇOIS

Let's hope. Let's hope, still. But I need a moment of rest. My legs barely support me.

JÉRÔME

Oh, no, no, don't halt, François; not when the blood is exhausted, like me, by weariness and hunger. Rest is a terrible danger.

SATURNIN

It's true. I've seen companions of misfortune stretch out like you yourself are doing. "We want to sleep," they said. And passed from sleep to death.

FRANÇOIS

Don't worry. Let me gather my wits; let's think of them, our poor wives from whom we separated in order to find them a bit of food and shelter.

JÉRÔME

Alas. Would we could rejoin them! We are lost, lost in this desert.

FRANÇOIS

I'm the one, I'm the one who caused your misfortune, your death.

SATURNIN

Why, no, no.

FRANÇOIS

We followed our army corps during this horrible defeat. My wounds haven't yet reopened and Marie stopped with me. You and your wives didn't want to leave us. And now see how we've lost sight of our companions and our flag.

JÉRÔME

And today I'm the one who led you far from our wretched wives. I thought I saw smoke from a hut. You followed me. And the wind came and the snow, wiping away all traces of our steps, and I no longer know how to orient myself to return to those unfortunates who are waiting for us, who are getting desperate, dying, maybe.

SATURNIN

Come on, François— Stand up! Stand up! We must try to rejoin them!

FRANÇOIS (in a weaker voice) Yes, yes, we must. I want to. I cannot, my friends, I cannot.

SATURNIN

What are you saying?

FRANÇOIS

Wait, wait a little longer, and it seems to me that if I slept a few minutes

JÉRÔME

Sleep? Remember, François, remember—that's death.

FRANÇOIS

No, no—I feel better. Leave me here.

SATURNIN

But we cannot abandon you like this!

JÉRÔME

You can no longer march, François? Well we will try to carry you.

SATURNIN

Yes, let's try. Let's try.

(they try to pick him up, but cannot.)

JÉRÔME

Impossible! Impossible!

(they fall down beside him)

SATURNIN

This last effort has broken me.

(he collapses near François)

JÉRÔME (in a thick voice)

François!

FRANÇOIS (with effort)

No—no—don't pity me. I'm no longer suffering. I'm going to sleep.

JÉRÔME (in a weak voice)

Sleep. Oh, it's all over! Well—we won't leave you.

(he stretches out next to François)

FRANÇOIS (half-dead, but trying to push them away)

No! No!

MARIE'S VOICE

François! François!

FRANÇOIS (half-rising)

Ah! Ah!

LOUISE

Saturnin!

JEANNE

Jérôme!

JÉRÔME (in a weak voice)

It's them! Let's try.

ALL THREE TOGETHER

This way! Over here!

(But their voices are so weak, so feeble, that they fall back exhausted. The wind blows forcefully, and the snow covers them from foot to neck. A silence. Then a small cart enters, dragged by a horse, led by a soldier on foot. In the cart are Marie, Jeanne, Louise, and Madame Wolf. They pass by.)

LOUISE

You were mistaken; they didn't hear us.

MADAME WOLF

Alas, no.

MARIE

Stop a moment. We must call again. François!

JEANNE

They never respond to our cries.

MARIE

It's impossible that we won't find them.

(The three women shout again. François, unable to speak waves his hand.)

MADAME WOLF

Let's keep going.

(The soldier takes the horse by the reigns. The cart distances itself. François falls back after a weak cry that no one hears. A new silence. Wolf appears.)

WOLF

I've followed them for the last four days without daring to show myself. If she saw me my mother would curse me again. She would refuse to be helped by me. And yet, I cannot abandon her. And why did she leave with them, with my enemies, with the man who crushed me with his generosity?

(looking)

They are far away. Let's go!

(starts to follow them, stops at the sight of François, Saturnin and Jérôme.)

More victims. More unlucky ones killed by this frightful climate. But I wasn't mistaken. It's them, François and his two friends! Have they ceased to live?

No—Jérôme and Saturnin are only numbed by cold and sleep. He alone is entirely frozen. He alone is dead. Dead. Why is my heart shaking—and my eyes are filled with tears? He was my most mortal enemy. Yes. But he spared me. Ah, I think he's still breathing! A little brandy may revive him.

(takes gourd)

That's all that remains to me not to die. Who care! He gave me mercy, and he's the support of my mother.

(pouring Brandy in François' mouth)

His heart.

(placing his hand on François' heart)

It's beating with greater strength.

Oh, these rags barely cover him. Come on, I am stronger.

(taking off his jacket)

"If heaven causes us to come face to face again, kill me if you can."

(covers him with his coat)

Here's my response, François. Heaven has reunited us. Your charity has germinated in my heart.

FRANÇOIS (raising a little)

Who's this by me? Who's this helping me?

WOLF

It's me, Wolf!

FRANÇOIS

Frédéric Wolf!

WOLF

Yes, and I beg you not to reject the help I'm giving you.

FRANÇOIS

Helped—by you! Alas, too late, too late. Marie—my—

WOLF

Marie—your wife—my sister now—my sister.

FRANÇOIS

Take her my last goodbye, my last thought. Your hand, my brother. Your hand—oh!

(seeing Wolf has removed his coat, he rises and returns it to him)

WOLF

Oh—think only of yourself. And you, Jérôme, you Saturnin. Wake up. Help me revive him, right away.

(Saturnin and Jérôme half wake up)

FRANÇOIS

You see, they, too, want to sleep.

WOLF

Ah, if your soul is not itself numbed, if your brain isn't frozen, if you can say, "I will," you can get up and march again.

FRANÇOIS

It's over, Frédéric! A prayer! A prayer!

WOLF

A prayer.

(listening to the noise of steps)

Ah! I hear—I hear them coming.

(going to look)

French.

(returning)

French, my friends, French.

FRANÇOIS

Fr—Fr—

WOLF

And among them the flag.

(French appear)

Your flag, you hear? Your flag. Your child, my friends.

(He signals the soldiers to stop)

FRANÇOIS (rising up a bit)

The—the flag. Jérôme, Saturnin—the flag.

SATURNIN and JÉRÔME (stretching their arms)

The Flag.

SOLDIERS (going to François)

The Colonel.

WOLF

Wait, it's their soul that needs to reawaken; it's their energy that needs to be reborn.

FRANÇOIS (rising up again)

Yes—alas—there are barely twenty to protect it.

WOLF (aside)

Ah!

(aloud)

And the energy. The Cossacks are close by. And you won't be there to defend it.

FRANÇOIS

Ah, if I can.

(raising himself and leaning on one knee)

And you, Jérôme, Saturnin—a last effort, recall your memories, and your energy—will revive at its sight.

The flag, it's the soul of soldiers, it's the village clock which marches in the middle of a regiment, it's the family, it's the absent homeland. Under the flag, it's still France.

(saying this, he supports himself with the flagpole, which he leans on. Saturnin and Jérôme crawl towards him.)

JÉRÔME

Yes, yes, France.

SATURNIN

France.

WOLF

They are saved.

ALL

They are saved!

(Shots heard in the direction taken by the women in the cart. The cart returns followed by Antoine, Molinchon, Boudinier, and others. Molinchon is the last firing at the enemy.)

MOLINCHON

Got another one. That makes fourteen for me.

FRANÇOIS

Marie!

THE WOMEN

Ah, there they are! There they are!

MOLINCHON

And here come the gentlemen Cossacks!

ALL

The Cossacks!

FRANÇOIS

Comrades, surround the women and the flag and we will know how to force a passage.

ALL

Yes, yes!

(They form a battalion. The Cossacks enter shouting "Hurrah!")

COSSACK LEADER

French, you are surrounded on all side, put down your weapons and give up.

FRANÇOIS

You hear, my friends. They propose we surrender. To reject our past, to trample our honor under our feet, and give up our dear flag. You know my reply in advance, and I'm going to sign it with my blood. Make yours now.

MOLINCHON

That's the way it is, Captain.

(going toward the Cossacks)

Surrender to you, to Cossacks?

Hold on, if Cambronne were here, he'd tell you what I'm thinking.

COSSACK LEADER

Ah, so that's the way it is.

(He shoots at François. Wolf hurls himself in front of François, taking the bullet, and falls.)

MADAME WOLF

Frédéric, my son!

FRANÇOIS

Wolf!

WOLF

Don't pity me, mother. It's expiation. I've bought back my past. I'm going to join my father.

(he dies)

ANTOINE

The Cossacks.

FRANÇOIS

Forward!

(The Cossacks and the French survivors fire on each other. French soldiers attracted by the gunfire arrive. The Cossacks retreat. The French surround the flag, shouting, "Long Live France!"

CURTAIN

SCENE X

The court of the Prefecture of Grenoble.

ANTOINETTE

This is the place we must present ourselves, they said.

MOLINCHON

Yes, it's the prefecture of Grenoble. Here's where the civil authorities will receive us and reincorporate us.

ANTOINETTE

Well, let's go in. But which side is it?

MOLINCHON

That way, doubtless.

(as he starts to go in, Boudinier emerges)

ANTOINETTE

Ah, bah!

MOLINCHON

Mr. Boudinier.

BOUDINIER

To whom do I have the honor to speak?

ANTOINETTE

What do you mean! Do I have the honor? Why, it's us, Antoinette.

MOLINCHON

Yes, it's us. Molinchon.

BOUDINIER

Ah, yes, yes. Molinchon, Antoinette. I recollect.

ANTOINETTE

That's fortunate. You still owe me for six glasses of rum for which I gave you credit from Moscow to Smolensk, and in those days it was worth ten francs each.

BOUDINIER

These days it's worth six sous for all six.

ANTOINETTE

Six sous!

BOUDINIER

Here's what you're due, Madame, and I don't ask you for a receipt.

(to Molinchon)

And you, Mr. Molinchon?

MOLINCHON

As for me, I loaned you nothing; on the contrary, I received something for you.

BOUDINIER

You received?

MOLINCHON

A lance cut that a Cossack wanted to pay you. But it seems you didn't have time to get it. You turned your back and I got it in your place.

(pointing to the scar on his face)

I paid him off. Here! But don't worry, the Kalmuk—and he has nothing more to claim.

BOUDINIER (worried)

Ah, yes, yes, I—I see.

MOLINCHON

Whenever you like, Mr. Boudinier, I will reimburse you for

what I received on your account.

BOUDINIER

Thanks, no thanks! I hold you quits.

MOLINCHON

Indeed, indeed, it's a small matter to settle, and you will choose the coin.

BOUDINIER

Wh—what coin?

MOLINCHON

Yes, sabers, swords, pistols. I have no lance to offer you.

ANTOINETTE

Well what do you choose?

BOUDINIER

I choose—persuasion.

ANTOINETTE

Persuasion!

MOLINCHON

What kind of weapon is that?

BOUDINIER

First of all, I request to explain myself. I was wrong not to recognize you, and I recognize that.

ANTOINETTE

Oh—

BOUDINIER

Yes, I recognize you, my friends

(low)

And it wasn't ingratitude that made me speak as I did. It's—a funk

ANTOINETTE

A funk!

BOUDINIER

What funk? Since the entry of the Allies into France we are living under a regime of suspicion. I'm afraid of these people, you see— And so they won't harm me, I've placed myself with them. I'm an errand-boy in the Prefecture.

MOLINCHON

You're afraid, you—you, Mr. Boudinier, you, the brave Boudinier!

BOUDINIER

What, my poor lad, you find yourself again in the basket of my protection.

MOLINCHON

Why, damnation!

BOUDINIER

Well, it will be a fine day when I don't offer it any more.

ANTOINETTE

For me, too.

MOLINCHON

Come on, will you. Don't I know your courage.

BOUDINIER

I no longer believe in courage, it's an illusion which is quickly dissipated. Yes, my poor Molinchon, I'm a coward—like the moon. I hold the snail for the race to glory, and the wild jack rabbit to leave the field of glory.

MOLINCHON

It's not true!

BOUDINIER

For all that, I'm not a bad sort, nor an ingrate.

(with emotion)

I have some heart, you see, and I haven't forgotten what the two of you did for me. Oh, no. I have not forgotten! Antoinette, it's not ten francs a piece your little glasses of brandy are worth, it's ten thousand a piece, since without them, I would be dead.

(weeping)

There were six. That makes sixty-thousand francs that I owe you, Antoinette.

I earn twelve thousand francs per year at the Prefecture.. I will deduct a hundred sous per month until I've paid you the whole sum.

MOLINCHON (shaking his hand)

Ah, ah—that's really good.

ANTOINETTE

No indeed, no indeed, I don't want it.

BOUDINIER

As for you, Molinchon, I ask nothing for what you received, it's I who owe you, on the contrary, and if I can, I'll pay you off.

MOLINCHON

Thanks, my brave Boudinier.

BOUDINIER

No, no. good, Boudinier.

MOLINCHON

Well, I really want that my good—brave, Boudinier.

ANTOINETTE

He won't let go his hold.

ANDRÉ (entering with Marie)

Keep hoping, Madame, hope.

ANTOINETTE (low)

It's Madame Beaudoin.

MOLINCHON

Madame Colonel.

MARIE

Hello, my friends.

ANTOINETTE

Well, Madame, you didn't learn anything?

MARIE

Nothing.

MOLINCHON

Our poor Colonel.

MARIE

Alas, I have no more courage! Why have they separated me from my husband? Whatever may happen isn't my place with him?

ANDRÉ

It's at Smolensk you told me that this separation occurred?

MARIE

Yes, it was at Smolensk that the Emperor trying to reestablish discipline in the wreckage of the army placed the women and the wounded in the rear guard.

BOUDINIER

The rest of us were in the rear guard.

MOLINCHON

Me, because of my wound. Antoinette, because she's a woman, and Mr. Boudinier as an apothecary.

MARIE

Some time later we crossed the Beresina, the army, harassed by the enemy was cut up, once again. And Jeanne, Louise and I, after terrible troubles, after unheard of sufferings, arrived in France. But we arrived there alone.

ANDRÉ

But since then, each of you has had news of her husband.

MARIE

Some soldiers who escaped death as we did, by a miracle, said they had met them, enduring with courage the harshest trials, and almost reached the frontier.

ANDRÉ

And as it is to Grenoble that remnants of their old regiment headed, you came to wait for them?

MARIE

Yes, or die, my friend.

ALL

Die!

ANDRÉ

What are you saying, my child?

MARIE

The tears, the privations, and the fatigues have wearied my body and my soul; a single thought, a single hope still sustains me: If François comes back, I will live. If he's dead why should I remain on earth? We've suffered too long together for one of the two of us to go to rest without the other.

ANTOINETTE

You'll see him again, Madame, you'll see him again.

MARIE

I know that perfectly well. But where? Here, or on high?

BOUDINIER

It will be here. Hold on, if you like, Madame, I'll take you into the offices. We will see if some news has arrived from Paris.

MARIE

Thanks, my friend.

ANDRÉ

Courage, child, courage!

ANTOINETTE

Poor, dear woman! It's like she says, if her husband doesn't come back, she'll go to meet him.

MADAME WOLF (entering)

Marie! Marie!

MARIE (turning)

Madame Wolf!

MADAME WOLF (trembling)

Yes, it's me, my child, with this brave Antoine, who's bringing you news.

ALL

News!

MARIE (very upset)

Of him, right, of him?

ANTOINE

Yes—yes, Madame, yes.

MARIE

He's alive? But where did you see him? Where did you leave him for the last time? When can I hope to see him again?

ANTOINE (forcefully)

When will you see him?

MADAME WOLF (low)

Be careful. You see how pale and weak she is.

ANTOINE

Well, when we left each other it was—it was at Leipzig.

ALL

At Leipzig.

MARIE

At Leipzig! That was still quite far away.

ANTOINE

It's true, but—we saw each other again—after—

MARIE

Ah!

ANTOINE

We met in Strasbourg!

MARIE

In Strasbourg, in France. Meaning, out of danger!

ANTOINE

Yes, the danger has ceased; all that remained was weariness, fatigue, and we were quite overwhelmed, when we arrived together in Paris.

MARIE

In Paris! You were with him?

ANTOINE

There we received the order to head towards Grenoble.

MARIE

He's coming, then? He's coming?

ANTOINE

Yes, Madame, he's coming. But as they told him, your health was weak, in need of care, he thought, this morning, that it would be better to forewarn you—

MARIE (beside herself)

This morning!

ANTOINE (very moved)

And he just sent me along first—just now—a moment ago.

MARIE

Ah, he's here—he's here—near me!

FRANÇOIS (calling)

Marie!

(Enter François, Saturnin, Jérôme, Louise, and Jeanne. The three soldiers are dressed in tatters. Their faces show the imprint of their long suffering.)

FRANÇOIS

Marie! Marie!

MARIE (throwing herself in his arms)

Ah—I see you again, I see you again!

FRANÇOIS

My poor Marie! How you must have suffered! And I wasn't here to support you.

MARIE

And you, covered with wounds.

FRANÇOIS (pointing to Jérôme and Saturnin)

I had two good friends, two friends—it's because of them I'm still living.

MARIE

How can I ever repay you—?

JÉRÔME

Heaven discharge the debt; it returned Jeanne to me.

SATURNIN

And it gave me back Louise.

ANTOINETTE

Don't you have a little word to say to us, Colonel?

FRANÇOIS

Antoinette!

JÉRÔME

And Sergeant Molinchon.

SATURNIN

And Mr. Boudinier.

FRANÇOIS

We are very happy to find all of you again.

ANDRÉ

All! Even old André?

ALL (astonished)

André!

ANDRÉ

You don't remember. It was eighteen years ago. I was already an old geezer, a poor proscribed priest.

FRANÇOIS

Wait. I do recall. I recognize you. It was you who blessed our poor flag.

ALL

Him!

FRANÇOIS

You predicted a glorious future for it.

ANDRÉ

And what glory has been more dazzling?

FRANÇOIS

But the time of misfortune has arrived for it.

ANDRÉ

Say a time of tests.

FRANÇOIS

Our flag! You recall, André, the beautiful day of its birth, and you, friends of its baptism at Arcole—of its glory in the whole world. Alas, here it is, proscribed in its turn, now.

ANDRÉ

Yes, proscribed. But what's become of it, what have you done with it?

FRANÇOIS

Our eagles, our flag, the enemy couldn't choke it out of us. Some braves, before expiring, hid it under the snow; others buried them in the soil, or wrapped themselves with them, in that glorious winding sheet.

ANDRÉ

But yours? Yours?

FRANÇOIS

The one that was blessed. That one must survive.

ANDRÉ

You kept it?

THE THREE OFFICERS

Yes, yes!

ANDRÉ

Lower, speak lower. You said it was proscribed in its turn.

SATURNIN

What's the matter? Is it not permitted to me to wear on my breast a blade of red-material.

(he opens his shirt and reveals the red of the flag.)

JÉRÔME

Is it forbidden for me to cover my wounds with this piece of white silk?

FRANÇOIS

And as for me, don't I have the right to wear this shirt?

(They stand together and form a tricolor)

MOLINCHON

Hell's bells! It's our flag!

BOUDINIER

It only lacks a pole.

ANTOINETTE

The pole and the eagle.

JÉRÔME

The pole? It's my traveling stick.

(pointing to the stick he holds)

And the eagle—

(pulls it from his pocket)

ANDRÉ

My friends, I have a prayer to address to you.

ALL

A prayer.

ANDRÉ

Allow me, in my turn, to give you asylum.

FRANÇOIS

You?

ANDRÉ

They won't come looking for you at my place. Not to an old geezer who they'll suspect of political conspiracies. Give it to me.

FRANÇOIS

But—

ANDRÉ

Don't worry. I know one must speak low of a return which is not impossible. Well, confide this noble wreckage with me. You will find them all again, the day when they must be rejoined—to make them fly in the face of the enemy.

FRANÇOIS

No, indeed; no, we mustn't permit—

ANDRÉ

Silence!

(André hides the flag in a pocket of his jacket)

BOUDINIER

The Prefect.

PREFECT (entering, to officers)

Gentlemen, you are not too late to have a share in the cadres of the army. The Minister has directed that the Regiments sent to Grenoble be brought up to strength. Many officers will miss the call, each of you will replace them according to his rank. I am expecting, right away, in this courtyard, the remnants of the 12th Regiment of the line.

ALL

The 12th Regiment!

FRANÇOIS

Ours!

PREFECT

Yours, gentlemen.

FRANÇOIS

Yes, sir. We were all three officers of that regiment.

PREFECT

Your name?

FRANÇOIS

François Beaudoin, sir.

PREFECT (removing his hat)

Colonel, your return is a great joy for us, for your regiment, for

France.

FRANÇOIS

I thank you, sir,—in my name, and in the names of my two friends, Captain Jérôme Leroux, Lieutenant Saturnin Renaud.

PREFECT

Gentlemen, you'll retain your old positions.

ANTOINETTE

Excuse me, Mr. Authority, and what about my job? Canteen lady? Don't I keep it? Don't they still drink in the regiment?

PREFECT

Indeed, indeed, brave canteen lady.

(drums can be heard)

And hold on, here's your regiment coming.

ANDRÉ (low)

Come, my child, after this review I will come back to find your husband, and I will bring him to you.

FRANÇOIS

Soon, I will go find you.

ANTOINETTE

Till later.

(Antoinette, Marie, Madame Wolf, André leave. The Regiment enters from the opposite direction.)

MOLINCHON

The Devil! I'm rushing to my rank!

BOUDINIER

As for me, I'm flying to my post.

(going into the Prefecture)

FRANÇOIS

My brave companions! How my heart beats in seeing you.

PREFECT

Colonel, grant me the honor and the joy of announcing your return to them.

FRANÇOIS

Do so, sir, but in the name of heaven, make it quick!

PREFECT

Soldiers! You are coming here to bring your cadres up to strength. You will receive with respect the new leaders you will be given, you will see with joy the former one who will be returned to you. Soldiers, among those you wept for are three that heaven saved.

OFFICER (at a sign from the Prefect)

Port arms.

(The regiment goes to port arms)

Lieutenant Renaud, Captain Leroux, Colonel Beaudoin. Your companions in arms salute you.

(The three officers remove their hats)

ALL

Long live the Colonel!

FRANÇOIS (weeping)

My friends, my dear comrades. After so many sufferings, so many struggles, after immense misfortune struck what we loved so much.

PREFECT (low)

Colonel.

FRANÇOIS

After such a misfortune, I see you again, and I cannot find a word of joy—I—I have only tears.

(Antoine approaches, rifle in hand.)

ANTOINE

That suffices, Colonel. We know—you don't need to say it. We understand. That's enough, Colonel, that's enough.

MOLINCHON

Well said, Antoine. You are furiously eloquent.

PREFECT (to an officer)

The flag!

(the officer leaves)

SATURNIN and JÉRÔME

What's he say?

FRANÇOIS

The flag.

(The officer returns carrying a white, Bourbon flag. The three friends join hands.)

PREFECT

It's to you, Colonel, that belongs the right to give it to your regiment. To you, to receive the oath to the new standard confided to your care.

FRANÇOIS

To me, to me, sir?

PREFECT (presenting him the flag)

No doubt about it—

FRANÇOIS

Oh! Don't ask that of me.

PREFECT

What do you mean?

FRANÇOIS

I cannot, sir, I could never do it.

PREFECT

What are you saying?

SATURNIN

You are right, François.

PREFECT

Come on, come on. It's your duty, Colonel.

FRANÇOIS

My duty! You want me to swear fidelity to this flag. But I took that oath to a different one. It's the only one that I know, sir. Don't insist that I present them with that.

ANDRÉ (who's returned, goes to François, speaking low)

François, take care.

PREFECT

Colonel, think what you are doing.

ANDRÉ (low)

Think that he might return and you must be there to serve him again.

PREFECT

Hasn't this standard been the standard of France for centuries?

FRANÇOIS (to Saturnin and Jérôme)

My friends, what shall I do? Speak to me, advise me. It seems to me it's a crime, it's treason, a cowardly act they all are asking me to commit.

PREFECT

Sir, I respect your sentiments of honor and fidelity, but for a soldier there's no other standard than that of his country. Take it, then. Sir—it's now the standard of France.

FRANÇOIS (taking the flag with a trembling hand)

My friends, my brave companions in arms, you who, for fifteen years fought at my side—

(uttering a cry)

No—no! They will regard me as a coward if I present this flag to them.

PREFECT

Colonel!

FRANÇOIS

Let them arrest me, let them judge me, let them kill me. I will never be a traitor or perjurer to my oath.

(he rejects the flag)

Long live the Emperor!

PREFECT

Wretch!

FRANÇOIS

Long live the Emperor!

PREFECT (who has seized the flag)

This is the way you wanted it, Colonel.

FRANÇOIS

I accuse no one, sir. I know the fate which awaits me. I am ready to submit to it.

JÉRÔME

We won't leave you.

SATURNIN

No, no!

SATURNIN and JÉRÔME (taking off their hats)

Long live the Emperor! Long live the Emperor!

(Holding hands, they are led away by guards who surround them)

CURTAIN

SCENE XI

Beneath the walls of Grenoble.

ANTOINE

Condemned—they've been condemned!

ANTOINETTE

Yes, they found judges to pronounce the sentence.

ANTOINE

And they must be executed this very day. Here, under the ramparts.

ANTOINETTE

What—is there no hope? They are lost without resources?

MOLINCHON

Who's lost? Our three officers? Not yet, Antoinette, not yet.

ANTOINE

What do you mean?

ANTOINETTE

What are you saying?

MOLINCHON

And it's to brave Boudinier, to the heroic Boudinier, that we may owe their salvation.

ALL

To him!

BOUDINIER

No, indeed, no, indeed! Imagine—

MOLINCHON

Let me speak here. Here's the thing. We were in the court of the Prefecture, when they brought a paper for the Prefect. "Yet Another one," cried Boudinier. "Another what?" I said. "Another dispatch. It's the fifth one to arrive from Gap. The Prefect is absent. The Secretary who receives them just yelled, "Is it possible the Emperor is returning from Elba?"

ALL

The Emperor!

MOLINCHON

Yes, the Emperor! That news electrified me, as the saying goes. And, it gave me an idea. I rushed with Boudinier into the office of the Secretary. He said, "What do you want?" "The dispatches," we replied, "The dispatches, and be quick about it!" The Secretary refused. As for me, I raised my voice, and I noticed, I noticed Boudinier getting pale—with rage. The Secretary looked as if he would ring for help. I put my hand on my saber, and I saw Boudinier trembling with fury. "Don't waste time," he yelled. "The papers, damn it all!" And that's when I unsheathed. Boudinier no longer knew what he was doing as I put my sword's tip at the Secretary's throat. Boudinier, in his rage rushed to the door—to lock the enemy out. And the Secretary in a state of shock at last gave us the dispatches.

ANTOINETTE

And they announce the return of the Emperor?

BOUDINIER

Absolutely!

MOLINCHON (showing the dispatches and reading them)

Here they are they are all from the Mayoralty of Gap. Number One, The Corsican Ogre—

ALL (with indignation)

Oh!

MOLINCHON (reading)

Hold on! "The Corsican Ogre has disembarked on the Gulf of Juan. The population has risen against him—"

ANTOINE

And then what? And then what?

MOLINCHON

Number Two. "The usurper" already he's no longer an ogre. "The usurper is at Cerenen. He's tracked everywhere."

ANTOINETTE

That's a good one, that is. Then what?

MOLINCHON

Number three. "Bonaparte—Bonaparte has appeared at Barème, followed by several soldiers." Number four. "The former sovereign is headed toward Digne, escorted by a very large number of soldiers and peasants."

ALL

At last!

MOLINCHON

The last one, number five. "His Majesty, the Emperor and King has just made a triumphal entry into Gap, amidst the acclamations of his loyal subjects and is marching on Grenoble."

That's what we owe to this brave Boudinier.

BOUDINIER

No, no. To Molinchon.

MOLINCHON

Yes, good, brave—good Boudinier.

BOUDINIER

Decidedly, he insists on it.

ANTOINETTE

Will he get here in time to save them?

ANTOINE (To Molinchon and Boudinier)

An idea—my friends—I need a horse, quick, right away.

BOUDINIER

A horse—but—

MOLINCHON

We will find one. The first horsemen we meet we will force to dismount, the brave Boudinier and I will bring you his horse.

ANTOINE

Let's go quick. Not a minute to lose.

(great shouts outside)

ANTOINETTE

Look there—down there—in the midst of that crowd. Why—it's—

ALL

It's him!

ANTOINE

(pointing to soldiers emerging from the town)

And on this side a party from the garrison.

ANTOINETTE

Would they dare to order soldiers to march against him?

(The Emperor enters followed by Bertrand, officers, and grenadiers from the isle of Elba, carrying a tricolor flag.)

ALL

The Emperor!

NAPOLEON (uncovering his breast)

Yes, me. And if there's any among you, if there's someone who wants to kill his general, his Emperor—he can. Here he is.

ALL

Long live the Emperor! Long live the Emperor!

(All rush to Napoleon and kiss his hands. Others, the sleeves of his coat. Napoleon waves to Antoinette who gives him a snappy military salute in return.)

ANTOINETTE

Ah, Hell's bells—he recognized me. He said Hello!

NAPOLEON

I knew that France was unhappy. I heard its groans, its reproaches, and I've come back, My rights are only the rights of the people. I intend to reign, to make our beautiful France free, happy, and independent; I intend to be less its sovereign then the first, the best of its citizens.

ALL

Long live the Emperor!

MARIE (running with Madame Wolf to the Emperor, in despair)

Sire! Sire!

NAPOLEON

What's the matter?

MADAME WOLF

Sire, your bravest officers, Colonel Beaudoin, his two friends, his two brothers in arms—they're going to kill them.

NAPOLEON

Kill them! For what crime?

MARIE

The crime of fidelity to the Emperor.

NAPOLEON

Run! Run!

(Bertrand goes to leave. A discharge of muskets is heard.)

MADAME WOLF and MARIE

Ah!

(s second discharge is heard)

NAPOLEON

That's not firing for an execution.

(acclamations from the town)

Hold on. Listen.

(Enter François, Jérôme, Saturnin, followed by Jeanne, Louise. The crowd accompanies them.)

MADAME WOLF and MARIE

François!

FRANÇOIS

Marie! The news of the Emperor's return saved us. The soldiers fired in the air, at the shout of "Long Live the Emperor!"

NAPOLEON

My brave soldiers! My brave companions in arms!

JÉRÔME and SATURNIN

Him!

FRANÇOIS

The Emperor! The Emperor!

NAPOLEON

That's how they were going to reward your devotion to France, your fidelity to your chief.

(Napoleon takes François' hand and shakes it with emotion.)

FRANÇOIS

Ah, Sire. May Your Majesty forgive me, but after so many sad emotions, the joy, the happiness of seeing you again, I cannot speak, I cannot tell you—

(Shouting)

BERTRAND

What's wrong?

ALL (a huge crowd emerging from the town)

Long live the Emperor!

MOLINCHON

Majesty, we couldn't locate the keys to the city, so we are bringing you the gates!

BOUDINIER (with energy, preceded by workers carrying them)

The gates! Here they are! Here they are!

NAPOLEON

Soldiers! I will return your eagles! I will return to you those flags which raised you—which may have been destroyed.

ANDRÉ (entering)

Not all have been, Sire. Colonel François, here's the one you confided to me.

NAPOLEON

Keep it! Soon, I will return it to the regiment with its brave Colonel. Until then, it will not be in worthier hands.

FRANÇOIS

Oh, yes, I will guard it with joy, this flag which lived with our life, which bears as we do, its wounds and its scars. Sire, in seeing you again today, I feel myself seized with an unknown trembling, with feverish intoxication. It seems that my soul reads in the future. I see these victorious eagles flying anew over France, and you, noble standard, be happy and proud, for the fate of battles has beat you under the ices of Russia; the God of Battles will raise you again, even over the Moscovite land, and our children, luckier than we, leaving the shores of the Seine, will see you one day floating gloriously beneath the sky of Italy.

CURTAIN

SCENE XII

The clouds open and vanish and reveal the plains of Solferino. Battle, and victory of the French.

CURTAIN

ABOUT THE AUTHOR

Frank J. Morlock has written and translated many plays since retiring from the legal profession in 1992. His translations have also appeared on Project Gutenberg, the Alexandre Dumas Père web page, Literature in the Age of Napoléon, Infinite Artistries.com, and Munsey's (formerly Blackmask). In 2006 he received an award from the North American Jules Verne Society for his translations of Verne's plays. He lives and works in México.

www.ingramcontent.com/pod-product-compliance
Lightning Source LLC
LaVergne TN
LVHW041616070426
835507LV00008B/269